D1161352

 *Southern Messenger Poets*

DAVE SMITH, EDITOR

Open Field, Understory

Open Field, Understory

new and selected poems by

JAMES SEAY

Louisiana State University Press
Baton Rouge and London
1997

Designer: Michele Myatt
Typeface: Granjon
Typesetter: Impressions Book and Journal Services, Inc.
Printer and binder: Thomson-Shore

Library of Congress Cataloging-in-Publication Data
Seay, James
    Open field, understory : new and selected poems / by James Seay.
      p.   cm. — (Southern messenger poets)
      ISBN 0-8071-2129-0 (alk. paper). — ISBN 0-8071-2130-4 (pbk. : alk. paper)
      I. Title. II. Series.
    PS3569.E24064   1996
    811'.54—dc20   96-36281
                                                    CIP

Poems herein have been selected from: *Let Not Your Hart* (Wesleyan University Press, 1970), copyright © 1967, 1968, 1969, 1970 by James Seay; *Water Tables* (Wesleyan University Press, 1974), copyright © 1972, 1973, 1974 by James Seay; *Said There Was Somebody Talking to Him Through the Air Conditioner* (Palaemon Press Limited, 1985), copyright © 1985 by James Seay; *The Light as They Found It* (William Morrow and Company, Inc., 1990), copyright © 1986, 1990 by James Seay. The author wishes to acknowledge the editors of the following periodicals, in which some of these poems, or versions of them, first appeared: *American Review, Carolina Quarterly, Georgia Review, Gettysburg Review, Kansas Quarterly, The Nation, New England Review, New Virginia Review, Southern Humanities Review, Southern Review, Virginia Quarterly Review,* and *Western Humanities Review.* "Tiffany & Co." first appeared in *Antaeus.*

   Of the new poems, a version of "Two Poems on Declension" appeared originally in *Chronicles* (March, 1991); "Deep in Dordogne," "On the Steps to Roquebrune," "Tidal Rivers," and "Where Cerritos Is" first appeared in the *Southern Review* (Autumn, 1994; Autumn, 1996).

   "Where Books Fall Open" was commissioned by the Institute for the Arts and Humanities at the University of North Carolina at Chapel Hill. *"The Puritan"* was commissioned by the North Carolina Museum of Art. "Clouds over Islands" and "Where Our Voices Broke Off" were published originally in limited edition by Deerfield Press/Gallery Press, Dublin, 1978.

   The author wishes to thank the American Academy of Arts and Letters for an award, the monetary aspect of which helped the writing of these poems. Thanks are extended also to Ruth Hettleman and the Institute for the Arts and Humanities at the University of North Carolina at Chapel Hill for a Hettleman Fellowship, which aided in the completion of this book.

The paper in this book meets the guidelines for permanence and durability of the Committee on Production Guidelines for Book Longevity of the Council on Library Resources. ∞

For Caroline

Contents

from *The Light as They Found It* (1990)

from *Said There Was Somebody Talking to Him Through the Air Conditioner* (1985)

from *Water Tables* (1974)

from *Let Not Your Hart* (1970)

Epilogue

❧ New Poems

The Fire of Both the Old Year and the New

At year's end my wife and I build the small fire
of whim that began one year when all the corks
we were saving for we knew not what (compost
or some other conserving gesture) came to mind.

From the couch we lob into the flames what remains
of our year's decanting, and the fire increases
cork by chosen cork until the room is soft glow
with what we imagine as pure residuum

of the wine itself, flame of first vapor respired
into the moist cork and now held desiccate there
in the one sailing across the coffee table
toward the fire of both the old year and the new.

One of the many pleasures here is the calling
again of the vintner's name and what we remember
of his sanguine gift, though that is not to suggest
it was all *vin rouge,* for there were the little whites

too, and blushes, whatever labels caught our eye
or won us to their cause by their truth in the mouth,
the cup of kindness, taken yet for auld lang syne,
but taken too for the small fire of the moment.

Nothing He Had Ever Thought or Done

I

What varied qualities of tenderness
can be summoned from memory of war,
I was thinking as Angus Robinson
came up the walk again in memory
with the Easter lily for my mother.
It was two years after the last world war,
and he had come to visit my father
with whom he had walked out of the ruin.
They talked through the night, and I feigned sleep
on the couch to hear of war my father,
for reasons of his own, would never share.
All the while, the faint scent of the lily
filled the living room, and my mother slept
her own sleep, rooms away—the sleep, I think,
of one accepting the gift of a man
smiling and whole, at the door, home from war.

II

If that is to glorify, by mention
of the human face in happiness, war,
I have not told my piece to good effect.
There was something tender too in the way
the fisherman and his small dog Hitler
held up the great blue tuna they had caught

and brought to market that day in Marseilles.
And I grant there are two ways we could go
with that: genocidal slyness veiled in
concertina-wire humor, or the joke
of one who doesn't know any better,
who knows only that the war is long gone
but that his dog manifests savagery
on those occasions when dogs go primal.
But for now the two of them are offering
this grand fish for sale, and the tenderness
I am telling you of may be discerned
in the complex passion of the moment.
It is evident in the shared regard
they have for the fish that fought and is dead.
There is commerce, yes, and no denying
the glory of scent working visibly
in the bristling of hair on the dog's back.
The sun has turned the blood to a brown crust,
but the *cozzo* has been cut from the fish
in a wedge that can be lifted to show
the fish's freshness and the fisher's skill.
It is not the passion of martyrdom.
There is human coin, and men drunk on wine.
But there is this man and his dog alive
with everything the day is giving them,
something that goes beyond food in the hand,
beyond what we know of the animal
in us aquiver, all this possibly
an event I am making too much of.
If there was no tenderness, though, tell me
it was the light on the water, the dark
flow beneath it that was life to the fish,

the keen sentience of the man and his dog,
my acceptance of the banal name,
the festival forming around the three,
the thing I felt between myself and those.

III

On Nevsky Prospekt in St. Petersburg
there is preserved on site a stenciling
still decipherable and almost quaint.
The Cyrillic characters stand in white
against a background of delicate blue,
and into the stone has been set a ledge
on which survivors leave flowers daily.
The stencil was once a warning to those
passing there that their side of the Prospekt
was subject to severe shelling at times.
Those times were known only to the Germans
surrounding the city in the long siege
that lengthened daily to a thousand days
and rumors the newly dead were not safe
any longer with the taboo broken.
What is tender here is the rose I saw
in trite and sacrificial crimson
on a postcard sent from a far province
and placed on the ledge, I guess, by request.

IV

The varied qualities of women's hair
were a subject of study for optics

used in bomb sights, and in crossing cross hair
with flowers and remembered names can I
leave to history my small catalogue
of amazement that we have continued
somehow this far to find available
breath and sound sleep for any night's comfort.
To help where she could, my wife's grandmother
cut sparingly the blond hair of her child,
my mother-in-law, for the war effort.
It was the unpermed and enduring strand
of feminine hair, specifically blond,
they found, that made the optimum cross hair.
The question taking shape in all of this
comes now in its unanswerable shape:
by the time the man bent to the cross hair,
what thought could he give to the living thing?
How enlist in this too the man and dog
who went out on the wide water to find
the fish whose spilt blood we on condition
can accept along with the war stories
of my father and Angus Robinson?
But I have no question regarding this:
when he came up the walk, the flower shone
and what he put into my mother's hand
was the gift of one who walked through ashes
for nothing he had ever thought or done
and now he had come to confirm his doubt.

Marigot, F.W.I.

The bad boys on the island pier,
or so one of them called another,
bad boy, with their monofilament line
and small bait, and then another, *bad boy,*
until they were all inscribed in the joke,
bad boy, what did they imagine
more than mere wink or brief toy
swallowing their tiny hook?
And why the handlebar,
isolate, no frame in sight?
Bad boys, barefoot on the pier,
raucous and limber against the bright
chalk of cruise ship,
brochure palm and sand, turquoise
sea, firmament, bad boys,
threadbare, shoeshine, chimney sweep,
small fish nibbling at their bait,
one of them, *bad boy,* motor-
mouth, mime of torque, miniature
jester in the realm of hard and fast,
running zigzag on the beach
with the uncontrollable handlebar.

HUNGER

Deer were the first to come,
nosing the faintly diesel breeze.
Our builder said they came to lick grease
from around the fittings on his dozer.
A season later we'd find pansies
shorn or uprooted and cast aside;
likewise the dahlia bulbs
I planted as a surprise for Caroline.
The teeth-marks looked almost personal
in the green tomatoes they teased and culled
from our first garden on the island.

But was that hunger gentle
in its penchant (the odd shot
of grease aside) for flower and fruit?
Inland a single herd
can ravage whole acres of corn.
Or any less urgent
than the rage of small teeth
that marked the plastic tops of garbage cans
we had to strap with bungee cords?
One raccoon had grown so bold
we were barely inside
before he hunkered out to sort
through bluefish heads, peelings, rinds.
It was a cross of hiss and growl
when we came upon him once
eating kraft paper we'd floured chicken on.

What does the heart home to, then,
when hunger, surrounded by water,
seems so magnified in its insularity?

Ah, little tree frog, toothless and brave,
you think you are the answer?—
thrumming inside our downspout
you've made into a summer home,
and so resonant in your chant
against the long drought?

Where Cerritos Is

for my son Page

So little did we know his Spanish
we thought he said Demente
when asked his name,
and it was under that outlandish alias
that Clemente worked as painter's helper
beside his friend Luis, whose moonlight bid
had brought the two of them to us.
Luis was too polite to tweak our Anglo ears,
knowing that his friend had no visa
or good reason to want to see Cerritos
so soon after the recent abrupt departure.
No hay problema, Luis later assured me.
Thinking, no need to trouble
the crazy gringo with too much explanation.
So they painted and sang the love songs
they loved to sing on the long runs
of lap siding, and on the ladder
reaching for the eaves, and in the bond
of tremolo radio stanzas from home.
It was the venison chili, though,
and the map, that got them talking,
and talking of home, Mexico.
They hadn't brought food,
and the closest we could offer
to what we thought they hungered for
was chili from the freezer;
the map was filler, show and tell,

where our words wouldn't work.
But, first, the goat;
the venison reminded them of that,
and Luis wondered aloud where he might find
such a goat as he had had at home, Cerritos,
not an old goat, for he is tough and fouled with piss,
but a young goat, tender and ready for the fire
that Luis and his friend, the one
we thought demented, Clemente,
would lay and put the pure meat of young goat upon,
and when we ate, they would point to the map,
clear in their mind where Cerritos is.

GIFT LIST

A distant relative of mine
(not blood kin,
and distant too in degree
of fondness my country cousins
and I—and secretly my mother—
could find for her
and her Daughters of the American Revolution
condescension),
Mrs. D. G. Hay at age 83
made a list I found decades later
in her birthday book of those who came,
and then a list of who had given what.
Ruth and Sara H., sisters I assume,
gave a *mist cologne;*
the *Memphis Norfleets,*
a *box of w. paper,*
either wrapping or writing or white;
Mrs. B. W. Wadlington, money,
and then, in penciled afterthought,
$5 dollars;
Tussy Midnight and *Midnite Tussy,*
one from *Ola & Theo Swango,*
the other from *Madge Doty.*
Probably *Alma Lemaster*
consulted with either Ola or Madge;
she brought a *Coty.*
A second *box of w. paper:*
Joe David- & Sadie Page;
an aunt and uncle I truly loved.

Many *lovely H'd'k'fs*—
Margaret Swango, Helen Fay Floyd,
Eloise Orr, Miss Boothe Weeks,
the list goes on.
As could my limning of it.
But toward the bottom
of the second column,
not far from the note
Bro. Fair and wife Cathy came
(shorthand for ministerial tightfist)
and just after Madge Doty's bottle
of *Midnite Tussy,*
I felt my amusement suddenly twist
within me and transform
into an almost ineffable
rending, the way joy and longing swept
the years and irony aside
and brought me my mother's face,
in her name there, and the listed gift,
Lucy Belle Seay—cake,
her given name miscast
in Mrs. Hay's crabbed hand,
but wholly light in all that came
off the page, Lucie, the cake in her hands
offered, the bread
of every day she had folded with light
and brought as a gift.

Flags

How we drifted heedless
under the fantail and flag of the merchant ship at dockside

is also the story of my father at war,
the conflation in my mind of those two flags

of peace and war. Something live in the water cutting through
the school of baitfish,

the altered pitch of gull cry, multiplying,
the shifting angles of sun and wind on water surface,

all this had gathered my friend and me to the bloodfeast.
From my small boat we cast lure after lure,

but whatever was feeding—shark, bluefish,
mackerel—wanted nothing we could offer.

And it was not until the sudden shadow
loomed that I looked up into huge Asian characters

painted on the stern, then saw the Rising Sun
popping in the wind of our drift.

Men on cranes were unloading lasered crates
I'd find on shelves inland.

What do I know of war
except that it came back in the equally sudden shadow

of grainy newsreels and my father's letters
that each beachhead

was worse than the one before
and he had not expected to get across the breaking shallows

between his LST
and the palms along the shore.

Years ago I would go to the attic and unfold
the souvenir flag of spun silk

he somehow sent from Okinawa,
its brown bloodstain

fresh in my mind from the dead soldier
he took it from.

Above us on the fantail was that same flag
and a Japanese seaman fishing from the rail,

casting and pulling in fish several to our none.
I gazed at him across economic zones,

newsreels, gulls diving into the frenzy,
and he could not have known

that I thought of cutting his line with my prop,
but that finally I waved back only because he smiled

and held up a streamer lure,
red and white, and what looked in the distance

like a gold hook, the sole translation
he knew, its feathers flickering in the wind like semaphore.

CISTERNAL ANECDOTE

According to my Uncle
Damon the only decent
cistern was double-lined,
the rock taken by hand
down into the earth and
placed piece by chosen piece
in the bell-shaped flare until there
was the double wall of stone for sweeter
water and self-respect. And when the reservoir
filled with rain off the tin roof, he took his sense
of what was decent and self-respecting one step more:
the single   goldfish   he slipped into the water
for the country summer. And naturally why and why one,
I asked. It feeds on mosquito larvae, he said,
and doesn't breed. Don't gag; it kept
the chosen drink of my summer
visits cool and clean and
I am here telling this.

Tidal Rivers

for Tim McLaurin, during transplant, 1990

When the black snake came calling today,
easing into the yard from the woods,
tentative, barely free from the ice of winter,
I hesitated, then took it as a sign.
There was after all the stark beauty of appetite,
the slight bulge of bird egg or field mouse,
and us somewhere along the line through phylum.
It may be that something in the hesitating
prompted the signal I sent—a single stomp on the deck,
my body language down through the treated pine
and out across the yard to where an old shape
was laying down its line once more
between the kingdom of the grass and what we are.
But mainly I wanted to see part of the miracle again,
the looping into the natural coil
so quick my breath would catch
between caution and the sheerest amazement
at how the same simple salts
fire the cells with their ions
to make the neural charge of survival—
that length of life, bright ebony, alert
to this hank of hair,
this standing-on-hind-legs one.
It was living closer to the bone,
coiled tightly against a shift in the flow,
the sudden elemental stir within,
and I want you to know that in all of this

I was thinking of you, thinking of how
you must now go deeper
so that every synapse of belief
will find its way through the riot
loose within your blood, so that the new marrow
attends, the graft takes hold.
      You told me once of the man you dreamed
who was trapped in a tidal river,
caught somehow in the tangle of his broken boat and motor.
Standing there in the rising tide
he reasoned that only by freeing a fuel line
and holding it in his mouth heavenward
could he survive.
It was a matter of holding the line upward and steady,
breathing in and out until the tide turned seaward,
hours away toward dawn.
There are rivers within our bodies
and they carry all that we are.
One river is the changing dream
of what we hope to mean.
Another is the one we sit beside
and think of our children.
Another is the flow of our hunger,
sexual, substantive, and light-seeking.
These are of course all one river and many.
For now they are that tidal river you dreamed,
and the man who held his belief in the air above
is taking the make-do windpipe from his mouth
and walking to the living shore.

Bridges

for Bascove

I

Water was the first motive,
then chasms of air
we needed simply to shorten
the distance across.
And what must the light
have been like in that water
once we could linger
in the leisure of suspension?
Toppled tree, braided vine.
And below us that likeness
of a clarity we had always sought
in mind's undefined stream.

II

I don't know what Lee Wayne Tucker
had in mind when he took the curve too fast
and came upon me and my army surplus jeep
halfway across the one-lane bridge,
unless it was how to talk
one nearby and not too particular hometown girl
into his ridiculous Oldsmobile and out to Sardis Dam.
At any rate, he put the jeep and me at a cant
against the frail railing where I hung stunned

until he came to offer his adenoidal assistance
and low brow, the flaxy, grease-laden shock of hair
and coital haze he seemed always lost in.
He didn't have insurance, and all Ivy Seales
the town marshall could get from him was a promise
to pay for the bent and totaled thing they towed away.
Not to put too fine a point on material things,
but I was young and dumb and some of what I thought of
as myself was in the hum of that jeep, open roof,
open road, with pals and girls of my own.
I got over most of that in time,
but what returns to me now and again
is how Lee Wayne just drove away
and when I'd see him later in some parking lot
or beer joint at the county line after work
he would tell me again how he was going
to make good on his word.

III

It is possible to confuse some of the saints
on the Charles Bridge with characters
from *Don Giovanni,* my friend Jaroslav
somehow told me as we crossed the Vltava
after an evening of vodka shots and pilsner.
That music runs deep in his life,
along with the stone saints on the balustrade,
and the words of books we tried to discuss
in broken English and French and even German
because I know no Czech, and my friend little English.
We had placed stones on Kafka's grave

and then visited with one of the old dissident writers
my friend shared a history with, a fervor of word and laughter.
But our laughter on the Charles Bridge that night
stilled as the two of us stopped to look into the river.
What were we trying to say to each other,
this man twenty years my senior, friend
and father figure in one? His body weight fell
to about 35 kilograms, he told me once,
and he thought he would die at the camp at Dachau.
I had to find a chart to factor the 77 pounds,
but like everyone I'd seen the photographs and footage.
And now I asked him if he thought about it much.
He shook his head and said it would bring bad dreams.
Then in nearly perfect English he added, smiling,
"After that, all was fish that come to my net."

IV

Surely the arch was first a dream,
how grace and strict economy
allows lateral stress
to be absorbed into the earth
by way of thrust,
granting thereby our suspension.
And there is too the sheer
making to consider, the bridge
of word or line
of sound, color, between
mind and world, our suspension
secured only as mind's thrust is borne.

LITTLE ONES, SCATTERED

Plume of air lifts me,
my metal glider,
but who's this . . . ? Bright swallowtail!

        Winter wren's nest-weave:
        white strips of print-out margin
        among twigs and straw.

Oh but unwise friend
has made her nest
in the roll of my bamboo shade.

        Old squirrel released
        from the mesh of my fish net.
        In my hand, heartbeat!

I would sting me too
if I found the mating call
was circle-saw whirr.

Two Poems Found in Old Programs

We Are Stardust

I'm looking at an old Fillmore East program
I got at a Procol Harum/Byrds concert in '69.
Down on Second Avenue at Sixth.
"A Whiter Shade of Pale," the Joshua Light Show,
Mary Jane, reefer smoke, whatever they call it now,
so thick we got high just sitting there.
At any rate, about four pages into the program
is a two-page ad for Woodstock, the *3 Days*
of Peace & Music poster with the little stylized dove
perched beside the hand on the guitar neck.
This was in late June I'm talking about,
and Woodstock was coming up in August.
Think of that, Woodstock hadn't even *been*.
And here it was for $7 a day, or $13 total.
Or nothing if you'd showed up at Max Yasgur's farm
in Aquarian innocence, thinking peace & music
and counting on the tents, water, restrooms,
and camping gear mentioned in the ad.
It rained so hard the first day that even Ravi Shankar
turned it in. I've never regretted missing that part of it,
the mud, or the bad acid trips and general slop of it all,
but just now I did put on an old Crosby, Stills,
Nash, & Young *Déjà Vu* to hear again
the way they unwind on Joni Mitchell's "Woodstock."
Tell me the truth, all the drugs and puerile flowers
and Vietnam and free love aside, when they hit that passage
about how by the time they got to Woodstock

they were half a million strong, and bombers turning into butterflies,
don't you want the whole simpleminded turmoil of it back?—
if for no other reason than to wail it out in total dumb abandon,
all three refrains, *We are stardust, we are golden*
And we got to get ourselves back to the garden.

Flat-Out, in 5/4 Time

in memory of Paul Desmond (November 25, 1924–May 30, 1977)

In signatures of time he was about
one figure short of death, and since
a friend of his had told me that, to watch
him waiting in the wings alone,
tweedling silently at what he'd blown
to us for years as alto kiss,
very nearly struck my small-town heart
in tablatures so sharp I'd bow
my head and weep in Avery Fisher Hall.
The date, my fading program says,
was *February fourth, nineteen seventy-*
seven at eight o'clock p.m.,
cold facts to keep me cool
as all my sentimental vinyl discs
so warped and worn I held my breath.
And when he bent in his embrace on stage
that night, the trill of blood and breath
I felt was youth come back again in love
with how that sound unwound in ways
unfound by words alone in space or on
this page of mine to try to tell

how Desmond came around at last to what
I had and had not waited for
because I knew "Take Five" would be his last
number of the evening and then
we'd have him only on the acetate
of studio recording sessions,
or albums grooving wider and wider
in riffs and licks he seemed to dream
from space and time you wouldn't think to count.
But there it was in lovely, wistful
solo, & defiant signature of 5/4,
the tune he wrote himself and yet
he'd wait in what I take as modesty
almost as Brubeck holds that final vamp
you think will never end until,
like a lover, and you know precisely when,
Desmond eases back in. This time
too the small *frisson,* the little soul-loft,
what the poet called catching joy
on the rise, the hint of flute and grape on the tongue,
but also knowing he was playing
while manic cells laid down their chords in blocks
so tight the wispiest tootle
would not be able soon to improvise
or find a way inside the chorus.
When his friend first told me of the cancer,
we were at Elaine's and Desmond
was talking quietly across the table,
glass and cigarette in hand,
and then his famous tune began to play,
the one I'd hold my breath to hear
at Avery Fisher Hall on down the road.

Routine enough, I guess, for some
that night, but I could not imagine fortune
smiling any truer, sadder,
on country mouse now come to city lights.
If he felt me staring dumbly,
he never showed the least rebuke or care.
In fact, he talked as though his tune
was not there, or anywhere, it seemed to me.
This then in memory of one
who blew his human breath into the horn
of life's good time and shaped in curves
a place his song could fill—and also tease
from silence, stop for stop, what count-
ed most: its counterbreath, another chance
to play for time, the song between.

THE PURITAN

in response to the statue by Saint-Gaudens

Wee must be knitt together
John Winthrop preached in purest metaphor

to those aboard the Puritan ship
Arbella, word and vision sure as apocalypse.

And that is what is easy to ignore,
looking at Saint-Gaudens' foursquare,

embronzed, and square-toed monument to dourness:
how their sense

of social covenant
informed so much of what we meant,

how intensely it was community,
and how by only sternest Liberty

in their narrow town
could we parlay the toehold of taken ground

into what we now call home.
Hawthorne spoke of a lamp

of zeal within their hearts, enriching all
with its radiance, and all was well

until the lamp began to dim
and then we saw their system,

how hard, cold, and confined it was,
he said, who surely knew them best.

In his tale "The May-Pole
of Merry Mount," you will recall

that iron Endicott
orders cropped the locks

of the bridegroom's hair who had gaily danced and wed
the Lady of the May. Even the trees turn sad.

But what invariably saddens me more
is when they shoot the dancing bear,

Puritans bent
on killing any merriment,

grim in their iron armor;
hard toil, he wrote, . . . *sermon and psalm, forever.*

Tell me, though, why do I pause
in the steadfast contractual gaze

of this bronze Puritan that Saint-Gaudens
casts before us, pilgrims?—

this early one who looks across the years
and makes discretion clear.

Too rigid still,
his sense of evil,

but of common cause his sense is firm,
what's now being knit into our fabric as a blur.

WHERE BOOKS FALL OPEN

It was not solely to test its heft
that I took the book's spine in my palm
and gave that slight downward gesture,
then let it rest;
rather it was in the way one calm
with the newborn will lift
an infant and do the same.
A way of welcome,
perhaps, but also maybe ritual
born of hope in what is gathered
there in signatures or swaddle.
At any rate, the book at hand
fell open to "Snow-Bound,"
Whittier's once-famous *winter idyl*
to what he called *the chill embargo*
of the snow, a week or so in his youth
when all the world he would know
was that of barn and hearth.
The thin line of wear along the length
of the book's fore-edge told where
reader after reader returned to hear
again the known measures of that winter storm,
the allure of the pull wombward,
as some might read it,
or the consonance of fire's gold with bourgeois habit,
or comfort of rest in one's assigned quarters
in the old patriarchal orders.
But this is to put too critical a point
on the simple literature of nostalgia.

Easier to accept it as heartfelt
yet innocent of how it gives us
only the no-surprises tour,
the driver of the bus
unloading the seemingly undimmed regalia
of time's little tea party in our honor.
Mais ou sont les neiges d'antan?
I think of where books fall open
to passages that promise that sojourn
at our chosen destination,
how it may be nostalgia's predictable return
or the alternative other, a passage rendering the known
familiar enough but at the same time
altering our sense of it, like *snow falling*
faintly through the universe,
and to follow that passage on out, *faintly*
falling . . . upon all the living
and the dead. Swoon is not too strong a term.
Nor at another time would doubt be—
or any word that tells of the changing dream
we have of the place, and the changing claim.
A final word, though, in the old poet's defense:
he spoke of the traveller who has *the grateful sense*
of sweetness near, he knows not whence.
Where then will our own book fall open,
and with what sweetness of the where we have not been?

Two Poems on Declension, One Loosely Rhymed, One Closely Reasoned

Won't You Be Mine, Columbine?

More than once I've dreamed of draping the skin
of an animal over my head and body.
I mean dreamed, in sleep, literally,
and trying to get wholly within.
As though I could trade
for a walk on the wild side
or maybe even *be* the feral thing.
At a party once way back when I was virgin-pure
and more or less clueless,
what is called an *older woman* in affairs
laughed and liked it when I got down on all fours
and put a pelt over my teenage head
and began to make the mythic sounds,
or so I explained to her, dramatizing my dreams.
Thinking about it later,
I realized she would have warmed to things
if I'd pressed for something other
than rubbing our hands over an animal skin
and talking the dream text
down to number, gender, and case.
That is, there was only the hint of sex
in her analysis and handsome Ivy League face.
Otherwise, it was pure and simple Jungian,
mythopoeic, hermeneutical syllabi.
In my case, there are tales that apply.

Like the one about the man
who couldn't find his ass with both hands behind him.
True, true, you push that skin thing too far,
you end up needing all your books and films
bound in leather.
Still and all, I'll always remember
the feeling I felt
when she passed her hand over that pelt,
still on my back, and asked how old was my mother.

The Reaching Back with Both Hands

Vector being both direction and magnitude,
I was thinking how the vectors of sex and money
converge with that of language and thus alter
both the arrow and force of how we talk.
Though his was primarily linguistic concern,
Varro once observed how *columba* served
to represent both male and female dove
until the breed became domestically blessed
and thus important in a minor financial way.
That's when the formal difference—
columba and *columbus*—was introduced.
He cites his aunt who sold five thousand doves
for a return of sixty thousand sesterces.
(To make sense of that, figure a sesterce was worth
about $\frac{1}{4}$ denarius or $2\frac{1}{2}$ bronze asses.
Big bucks in bronze asses.)
The birds were served at a single banquet.
Varro goes on to describe the ground plan of the aviary
as shaped like a schoolboy's writing tablet,

rectangular with rounded head.
I offer the detail to suggest
that to Varro it wasn't all academic.
By the time the flusher Romans
were finished with the *villa rustica,*
it was a pleasure dome.
They draped nature around their lives like skins,
the Roman coin talking turkey with pure pastoral.
So sooner or later little Mister *Sine Qua Non*
had to have a name of his own.
Otherwise who would have sailed the ocean blue?
Otherwise too what would we call the district
where our dominant politicians reside?
The patently feminine District of *Columbae?*
Moot point, I guess, there being so little chance
of gender confusion in the general declension of the place.
Maybe it's all finally phallephoric.
Or like what my sons used to say
when I asked them why a movie
they wanted permission to see was rated R:
sex drugs rock & roll,
the oldest declension of them all.

In Residence

If the old Slav is sad,
walking stooped and slow
to the end of the chateau's jetty,
is it because I found him
away from his desk
of translations, watching game shows
on the channel from Cannes,
or that the remote control
he is enthralled to
has in some way failed or confounded him?
Or is it because he breaks line at buffet
and suffers stares of wonder,
or that he eats
as through a hood,
and hoards wine at his plate?
Or is it the grayness of today's Mediterranean
following yesterday's azure
in the brief window of plenty
he has been awarded
for these three months of winter,
or the grayness of all his sweaters,
or his hair that was once bold?
Though they talked—with understanding,
it seemed—I do not think he saw himself
in the village drunk, who died last week
on the bench outside our gate.
And so it may be the weight
of one moment, the way the day began,
the bad dream carried over,

or something his father said too many times.
Or it may be that the skeleton of fence
and bunker at the jetty's end
has opened the album of far-off Sachsenhausen,
his barbed-wire house in 1941,
labor that almost set him free from breath.
It may be the hormonal tide falling slack
or simply the friendly note we all got,
reminding us in two days our residencies are done.
How he danced last night
in front of the big fire at our farewell dinner
and now is sad.
The picture he had me take—
him at his desk, manuscript in hand,
the fine room and windowed sea as background—
I couldn't be sure if it was a keepsake
or a flash of the cynical, saving Slavic wit,
something he'd share with cronies back home,
his photo joke of luxury on loan.
When I was sick from shellfish toxin,
he wrote a funny poem for me in French,
rhyming *comique* with *la bombe atomique*.
He wrote that the mussel is a little beast,
but soft, savory, and choice.

On the Steps to Roquebrune

There are small sharp stones
placed in the steps' patchwork mortar
for traction on winter ice,
and it is this detail underfoot and cinematic
that stops me on the steps to Roquebrune.
Not that I have forgotten her face or form
or that the years apart
have erased our years together,
but I did not think
to be broken away so sharply today
from the call of doves among cypresses
or the yellow of French mimosa in every garden.
We were here together once on unshared impulse,
the rented Renault already due at the station,
a train we couldn't afford to miss,
and I hurled us up these same steps
to find where the great poet Yeats
was buried in foreign ground
before his bones could be taken home.
Because we were trying one last time
to understand what we wanted to mean,
she went along, but I never found the grave.
Now these stones bring back that day,
the fits and starts of masked anger
and how we were trying to save the years together.
In an earlier town by the tour-worn sea
we had argued in a fury over nothing
more important than where to spend the night
or who would drive or when.

I wanted to watch holiday fireworks—
feu d'artifice—and the arrival of a beauty queen
named Stephanie Gomez, so I gave her the keys to leave.
At midnight when the little windmills of fire
whirled a finale above the chapel door
birds flew from their roost in the trees
and I tried to make it mean something,
sitting there with french fries and empty wine.
When she came back in the Renault
and found me on the curb,
I never knew if it was fear of being alone
on a foreign road or love that turned her,
but she gathered me into the car
and the road to Roquebrune.
Later on the train we had a sleeping compartment
and called it the love train.
On the path taken in memory of what is written
the sharp stones for traction on ice
mean no more than birds flying in the dark,
but deep in me I feel the cold hard thing again—
and also that quick feathering
by which we are lifted.
I stand here for a moment,
studying the weathering tiles
on roofs within reach,
then look out over the sea
toward where Stephanie Gomez
walked across the stage in sequins,
that fire of artifice lighting the night around us.

❦   from *The Light as They Found It*

When Once Friends

I can tell this fairly quick,
the two narrative lines sharing a common angle
and there being mist in both instances.
As for why my friend and I
were running a rented fishing boat
through morning fog on dead reckoning,
it was a matter of wanting to arrive early and alone
at the shrimp farm where sea trout
were working along the fence for strays.
More than anything I remember the angle,
something sure and strict in my reading,
of the cabin cruiser that came out of the fog
and crossed our bow close enough for us
to know again it was not our special selves
or anything our wives knew about greyhounds
that had paid us eleven-to-one on two-dollar bets
at the dog track the night before.
A name on the racing form more lyric than the next,
a combination of favored colors in the silks,
the worn luck of the draw,
were what bought us beer in green bottles
instead of cans for the weekend.
The cruiser never looked back
at my friend and me and our luck
rolling in their wake.
The other angle was of a plane in the clouds,
the only time I've ever been ferried by private charter.
Going up through cloud cover
the young pilot said he didn't have radar

and had never been to where I was going,
so we'd have to come back down through the clouds
in a calculated while and look around for a landmark.
His co-pilot pointed to a symbol
for a checkered water tower on the chart.
All I could add to the basic rhopalic of clock,
compass, and radio was another eye,
the one pointing my finger toward the Cessna
that had just slipped through the gauze
of our future like a cruiser
and laid down for the second time in my life
the providential angle.
Those twin incidents were long
ago and whatever has made
my friend remote and finally silent
as he goes about his days
is as hidden to me as the way two such moments
could conform so in texture and geometric circumstance.
One other thing:
after we found the water tower
and were parked on the runway,
the pilot walked around the nose of the plane
to where I was standing with my bags.
He reached up and broke a sleeve of ice
from the leading edge of the wing
and offered half to me.
His co-pilot had forgotten to fill the water jug.
After a few minutes of small talk
he taxied up the runway,
lifting into the overcast winter.
I stood there beside the one road leading in,
waiting for my ride and thinking of how the morning

cleared on the wide sound
and we caught the speckled trout
our wives broiled with pimiento and Parmesan,
lemon and parsley.
We drank the beer in green bottles,
saying the wonderful names of the winning hounds
all through the evening.
That was what I remembered that winter day
and what I remember now is both that and the angle—
and standing there on the small runway,
eating the ice of unknowing alone,
its cloud, where we had been.

Tiffany & Co.

for Elizabeth Spencer

Leafing through a friend's catalogue—
the Fall Selections 1987—
I linger on something the blue of a robin's egg
and wonder why I've never bought any of these *objets,*
never felt the specific fetish-force
of the commodity behind the revolution
of their brass doors or 800 number.
There's possibly history to explain:
we could go back, say, seventy years
to when my mother and JFK were born
and take a look around:
Freud's new Intro to Psychoanalysis on one hand,
Lenin entering the Winter Palace on the other,
but mainly there's the paradigmatic news
every winter day in Tyro, Mississippi,
of no indoor plumbing and a dead aunt's
five children extra to feed,
which lasted right on through my kindergarten
of visits to Granny's.
                    So why on Bolshaya Morskaya
would I go looking for Fabergé's old St. Petersburg shop
when where Lenin had breakfast
with smoldering Bolsheviks was just around the corner?
Well, maybe to have pissed into both the figurative
wind and a hole in the ground
is to be drawn to the abstract gloss
of privilege as though it might incorporate

and invite us to its private Mardi Gras—
such parades in life, for instance, as lunch
with the woman in Georgetown
whose every emblem was Camelot,
right down to sterling frame for the presidential scrawl
on a scrap of teletype
thanking her for the intro to Ian Fleming
and 007.
But it didn't seem, on Bolshaya Morskaya, the same dream
of Fat Tuesday's carnival and masquerade.
I thought of old Fabergé, Russian to the bone and in Swiss exile
while Bolsheviks, quit with eating fable-cake,
were already breaking rank and bellying up
to the tsar's bar, the monkey
of power settling on their backs,
jeweled eggs glittering in their words.
Power's not like Bond's regimental gin;
it wants to be stirred never shaken:
sooner or later there's the commissioned aria,
the room of shoes worn once or never,
cinema's kitten purr.
Or the threadbare velvet glove
on the stainless steel hand
the cautious in any century recognize.
                              She didn't smile—
my Intourist guide in Moscow—
but I meant it only as a joke
when I asked her if there was a tunnel
between the headquarters of the KGB
and the country's largest store of children's toys,
just across the street.
One imperial egg in the Kremlin nearby

still has as its surprise the miniature
Trans-Siberian Railway train.
Another opens to reveal Nicholas' yacht
scaled down in gold.
We have to imagine the crossties & rails, the constant steppes,
in all seasons, to the sea,
imagine the sea as well, and the globe
we want to shape and shape again.

Faith as an Arm of Culture,
Culture as an Arm of Narration

All those miles, the dark water beneath us
as we slept in the wide rows.
From Heathrow, jet-lagging and hugging the left
eight hours into the moors
to walk through the open gate
beside the flower garden and find it—
right where she said on the transatlantic telephone,
my friend Bonnie from Georgia,
away for the weekend with her fiancé in France:
the back door key
up under the mop bucket,
her grandmother's language and habit.

Time Open-Faced Yet Secret Before Us

for Roy, who thought he wrote
the book on bricks

I

One of the last places you'd look,
but it's there
on the floor between the wall and my stove:
a small digital clock
blinking hours and minutes
I'd probably fish out with gum or tape
if it weren't for the notion of time fallen
by chance beyond the senses almost and secret.

II

Even with watches
we lost all track of time
the time we drank all the high proof
rum we could find
and pour plain on ice in the clear jumbo plastic
cups the woman at the package store
in Crawfordville gave us when we crawled out
of the Wakulla wet and wild with our best
anecdote of the week.
All my buddies could shout about
was how the light and speed,

not to mention focus,
better have been right or I had
had it as captain even of my own craft.
I'd set the time-release
and slipped into the water with them
to look laughing into the lens
while the camera floated from us
on the bow of the boat.
At the very moment the shutter tricked
time for our yearly group portrait
dog-paddling in the middle of the river,
somebody looked around and found the alligator
surfaced among us, a confluence of events like no
other we could remember later that night
at the roadhouse restaurant eating fried shark
and beating on the table with the hilarity
of danger we were already hyping up for history.
And not a one of us could have told
the time, whether it was space
measured by time-honored points on our boat:
the bow being noon
where the alligator rose to our surprise,
or whether it was what we hoped had been
inscribed knot-eyed and ancient among us,
still secret in the chemical film,
or what the waitress,
weary with hearing our four-hour punch line,
weary with Hwy 98 driving the same
story all day and night
into Panacea Florida's penultimate
worst restaurant, said it was:
time to put the chairs on the tables, boys.

Of all my father has lost
since the war,
he told me he missed most
his photographs from overseas.
I think of his old Argus camera
hauled from island to island
in the pack with K rations and extra rifle clips,
as though each were needed
to validate the other.
Only the most disingenuous among us would deny
we want the light and speed
to be right
so that we shine in our fathers' eyes.
I don't know what else held us so
to the anecdote of danger,
but there was something outside the narrative
line, outside the hope of future proof
we had been there,
outside even the desired focus
of attention from another—
something close to living both
in the moment and in the option.

III

Not much was left
except the floor beams
and stone foundation by the time
we topped the hill on foot
two centuries later.
That, and a view time hadn't much touched.

She may never have forgotten
what she knew of England—
may have returned there
or gone elsewhere eventually—
but if the way she scanned
the Blue Mountains
in the green Jamaican distance daily
didn't come to be a permanent measure
in her dreams
I don't understand what's a lovely haze
of ridges and foliage rising
and falling in this world.
I'm thinking of the plantation owner's daughter.
She had first to get over the loss
of her mother, taken by fever soon after arriving,
and besides sickness there was unrest.
Even the favored house servants
stole away into the mountains
with the field slaves one night.
I am thinking, though, of their times—
father, daughter, fugitive
slaves, neighbors on the faraway roads—
along with us
outside the currencies of sugar and bananas
and fresh boatloads of blacks from Angola, Ghana,
wherever the world's sweet tooth bites sharpest.
I am thinking of how
at times the daughter
would go to the basement
and gaze into the brilliant day
or crescent moon through gun slits
her father had fashioned in the stone foundation

when it was laid.
I don't want her to sound
too exotic or romantically wistful.
While she had both the dreamy inclination
and an edge made keen by fine feeling,
she was capable of taunting
at least the younger blacks
and she more than once came close
to torturing cats in the cistern shed.
By the time we got there
it was all goats and ganja.
This was well off
what the travel brochures call
the beaten track,
and we wouldn't have been there
if my friend hadn't had a friend
who had needed an alternative
to his life in the States
and bought this goat farm
we could now visit.
He and his girlfriend gave us to understand
they sold only goats to the natives.
I remember their faces, sweet enough,
but not their names.
What lodges in memory is the daughter
and father's fallen-down house
we stumbled on,
the floorless mahogany beams above me
I wanted for my own,
and the gun slits in the stone foundation—
narrow vertical frames
beveled on the basement's interior side,

I remember, rather than on the outside
facing the surrounding mountains,
a slight architectural detail so pure
and simple that something of their lives
was given to me in a way
no page or moving picture could
without the very light around me—
something like an option
outside the lethal fact
of a bevel cut on the interior surface
of a wall to allow the widest angles
for their guns
yet not funnel, as an exterior bevel
would, what they had made
of race and station back
into their faces in the breach.
In my mind, his mind
and hand free almost of the imperial moment
and impulse, the chalk mark
on the stone for cutting, his letter
gone out across the North Atlantic
that they could book passage
to come in the spring.
But lodged more strongly
than any beveling for simple survival
is the message she left
in the enigma of metaphor
scratched years later beside one
of those same openings into the blue
In your chimney of love,
count me ten brick.
Tell me the measure, timekeepers:

stinting or taking the long view
that knows we are given so
widely to this world
that ten would be plenty
from any single hand pledging
to help hold warmth and focus what's not
needed into the blue.
But what do I know
of love or loss turned
to such a figure?
I can imagine her only so far.
It could have been a local
joke or private saying;
it could have been
ten clandestine days and nights inside
what passed for love,
or an announcement of minimal intent.
The chimney was gone
and our goat-farmer/ganja-man
knew of the house solely by rumor.
The view from the opening
she chose to leave her words beside
is the same as from the tall south windows
I imagine above,
but she is down here—
and not because there is danger.
For now, the smoke plumes of slaves
escaped to the mountains are domestic
in nature, and vague, simply part of the view.
I don't have anyone in mind for her.
There are these words
she wants someone to find—father

or lover?—and there is the optional
way in her mind space and time
are bordered and measured here.
Even with the roof and floor
vanished I see how
the dazzle of light is doubled in the small slit,
her time of love fallen by chance
before me almost, yet secret.
She is gazing toward the rise and fall
of ridge-line and clouds drifting inland
from the Caribbean,
her hand on the beveled stone
foreign and tentative
but alive with this
other way of being.

Clouds over Islands

First there was a dream not wholly mine.

I told my friends the dream
comes with the bed, its source a cloud
accumulated in the air surrounding sleep.

Just off the plane, I had dozed on their bed
as they swam in the screened pool, promising
I would like the crabs at Joe's Stone Crabs,
the daughter would be off the phone in my room
shortly, she was in love. The migrant dream
settled around me as the rhythm of the laps they swam
defined the rhythm of my breathing.

When I woke it took their voices
from beside the pool for me to know
I had breathed the dream
from the cloud above their private island of sleep.

The dream itself does not matter
in its particulars,
not even to my friends.
Nor could I have told it clearly, its cloud
so tropic and brief in my life.

I told them of a family I knew in Ohio
who bought the childhood furniture
of a famous astronaut, his little bed and mattress,

the strange vast air
in which the family's daughter began to dream.

Then together we remembered confusions
in the expired air over beds we had held
in hotels, hospitals, the compartments of trains,
or rooms of senility where our grandfathers called back
the gifts they had given us,
how sometimes still we rise from sleep in beds
where no friends have breathed dreams
we can enter without fear,
how we stumble to our belongings,
trying to make sure of what we left there.

WHERE OUR VOICES BROKE OFF

for Tom Huey

From the porch, if they hold to what there is
no need to imagine, they can color the hedge,
the sound, the lighthouse with its pattern of black
and white lozenges, or the air over the island
and anything lofted in its translations.
My sons turn their brushes instead to the chronic
bad dreams of the race, fixing them at random
in the watercolors of flame or collision.
They are old hands at apostrophe.
The shrimper's son from across the road tries a few circles
and then begins the outline of a boat.

Last night from this porch I looked up
with my wife and friends to our share
of the galaxy, whorled pure and free of mainland lights.
I felt our voices drawn out into the dark
and it seemed to me the round island was a stone
turning beneath us, grinding our voices with the shells
of shrimp in the kitchen pail, the quilts by the door,
the hyphens in the names of boats at anchor—all of it drawn
and turning under the stone—the drums of paint
for the lighthouse diamonds, the bright water that breaks
on shoals and jetties, whatever yields to silence, ground
with our voices and spread like grist across the spaces.

One of the Dippers brought us out of silence
and we began working our way through the known.

For the constellations we could not name
we imagined *Cricket's Knee, Bill & Doris' Blown Electric Range,*
Anne's New Rod & Reel, Tommy's Measles, and so on
until we all were found.
We called it the Myth of the New Understanding.
It was a way of turning from the silence beyond the porch
railing, the silence in the hedge along the road
and out across the sound to the lighthouse.
It was a way of understanding the lights
burning their codes through darkness.

The boat is colored yellow and the water blue.
It is headed to the left of the paper,
under what appears clear weather.
Toward dawn we saw his father make fast the mooring
and load his catch into a skiff.
I do not know if he looks up at the stars at sea
and wonders what is at the farthest reach of darkness
or if he dwells on whether the shrimp are vanishing.
I do not know if he has told his son of the silent migrations.
He declined the beer.
We bought the shrimp still moiling in the bucket.

What Words For

Bougainvillea, hibiscus, weeping fig?—
the Cuban let us walk along and point instead.
Leaving we looked like a rolling greenhouse.
There are larger terms for life and death, I know,
but wedged in the rearview mirror
among coolers of fish for the freezer,
Ficus benjamina was the one I fixed my hopes on.
Ficus, fig, whatever you want to call it,
the idea was it would somehow lift
the ailing one at home, its own genderless kind,
or, failing that, replace it in the cachepot
centering the living room window.
So we were something tropical
and self-commissioned coming north on I-95.
Part of the shading of tone, though, was how
our one-armed fishing guide had outdone us both.
But even with that nuance, ambient and humbling,
all the way from the Keys, it never dropped a leaf.

In all of this, the notion somehow our lives
are linked to them for more than the mere air.
There are reasons the Haitians
painted their small, almost toy, boat in bright stripes
of green and red and other reasons
they sailed it to where we had found it
confiscated and beached near Islamorada.
                        The ailing one at home,
for instance, I would falter
if it followed through on what sometimes seems

a drift toward barrenness or surrender.
For the move from Nashville thirteen years ago
I wrapped it in wet sheets
and then wrapped that in clear plastic.
I asked the mover if he would load it last,
in the rear of the van, and open the doors
halfway through June and the interstate to Carolina
for a little sun.

What I mean too is how they seem at times
to turn from us, a kind of judgment
they have no words for, only this dropping
of leaves, or that paling, from what has passed
through the room where it is not in the light
to be constant, how even now
the ficus that was green and flourishing
from the Cuban's smile, part of our cargo
of acceptable compromise and materiality—Igloos full
of cobia and dorado and redfish we would share,
the capital of a column I salvaged
from old resort architecture dumped against erosion,
a tarred hat with a Rebel Lures logo Made in Korea
we found in the tide—how even now
that one I saw something of the green future in
is turning and nearly sere.
Ah little sister, little brother,
children everywhere.

Inside, Outside, the Dialectics Once More

for my son Josh

How could we have known or cared with our tourist cameras
whether it was Sterno or Campbell's Soup?
The hook was how he had disconnected
the lights on the Christmas tree
outside the Church of the Heavenly Rest
and plugged his hot plate into the only extension cord
he could find in the east Eighties.
That, and maybe the fact our heads were full of van Gogh.
The cipher, that is, of the same hand holding and letting go:

we had wondered for hours at the nearly ninety canvases
of the final year and a summer,
seventy of them done in as many days, the numbers alone
a closure we couldn't shake off.
Like the others in the museum line
we looked for signs of ultimate intent,
the *suppressio veri* he had surely coded for detection
so that we would overtake him on the road outside Auvers
before he reached the suicide field.

But except for crows over a wheat field
we were left with olive trees and cypresses,
the great starry night, irises, two views of Daubigny's garden.
If most of that seems to spiral from cyclotrons
or strain toward fission like a vision of nuclear day,
consider its valency also in the way of life
coming back around to life in the constant cosmic charities.

So what was our evidence finally
but a further calculus of alternatives?

Another portrait of how we might be lifted and turned
was the Oriental woman high in the bell tower
on Christmas Day. I raised my camera once,
then let it drop unshuttered, the way her eyes were shut
and taking in the sun glancing off the river,
the way her hands rested
on the railing around the carillonneur's booth
as French and Dutch carols pealed from the tons of bells
and shook even the stones that held us there.

If the portrait seems a Zen cliché almost,
consider that I mean also the way Rockefeller millions
had put Handel finally in the air around us
nearly four hundred feet over Riverside, the way her coat
was crimson against her black hair, her butterfly bow
whimsical and silver in the winter light.
Consider that later as my son and I ate the sushi & sashimi
combination on Christmas afternoon, something
we had planned days before, we talked as much of the double-

square canvases van Gogh had turned to at the very end
or of photographs we might have had
as of anything Eastern or otherworldly.
One final turn, though: if our talk seems remote
from the events and unrelated to the chemistry of warm saké
or how as we walked out onto Broadway near sunset
the light was the light of boulevards and fields held
in the pledge of return, consider that we knew containment was not
those formal things alone, the way the world everywhere we found it

seemed something other than other.

Audubon Drive, Memphis

There's a black-and-white photo of Elvis
and his father Vernon in their first swimming pool.
Elvis is about twenty-one and "Heartbreak Hotel"
has just sold a million.
When he bought the house,
mainly for his mother Gladys they say,
it didn't have a pool,
so this is new.
The water is up to the legs of Vernon's trunks
and rising slowly as he stands there
at attention almost.
Elvis is sitting or kneeling on the bottom,
water nearly to his shoulders,
his face as blank and white
as the five feet of empty poolside at his back.
The two of them are looking at the other side
of the pool and waiting for it to fill.
In the book somewhere
it says the water pump is broken.
The garden hose a cousin found is not in the frame,
but that's where the water is coming from.
In the background over Vernon's head you can see
about three stalks of corn
against white pickets in a small garden
I guess Gladys planted.
You could press a point and say that in the corn
and the fence, the invisible country
cousin and mother, the looks on Elvis' and Vernon's
faces, the partly filled pool, we can read
their lives together, the land

they came from, the homage they first thought
they owed the wealth beginning to accumulate,
the corny songs and films,
and that would be close but not quite central.
Closer than that is the lack
of anything waiting in the pool we'd be
prompted to call legend
if we didn't know otherwise.
They're simply son and father wondering if it's true
they don't have to drive a truck
tomorrow for a living.
But that's not it either.
What it reduces to is the fact that most of us
know more or less everything
that is happening to them
as though it were a critical text
embracing even us and our half-mawkish
geographies of two or three word obituaries:
in the case of Kennedy, for example, I was walking
across a quad in Oxford,
Mississippi; King's death too caught me in motion,
drifting through dogwood in the Shenandoah.
As for Elvis,
there were some of us parked outside a gas station
just over the bridge from Pawley's Island
with the radio on.
That's enough.
I know the differences.
But don't think they're outright.
The photo is 1034 Audubon Drive, Memphis,
and then it's Hollywood,
still waiting for the pool to fill.

Not Something in a Magazine

It was intelligent enough, what the photographer had been saying
as I drifted out the door. Something about Susanne Langer on
   metaphor.
That there was as much for me in the moon and stars
tilting in the oval mirror I held at angles to the summer sky
is a measure of nights and days with so little glamour
I'd just as soon forget how I tried first to find my face
in the mirror mounted on the stranger's dresser,
left for some reason overnight in the yard across from the party I'd
   abandoned.
Yard sale, fresh paint, bad memories, I don't know why.
What I remember, after the cliché of self seen in shadow and
   silhouette,
is turning the mirror on its hinges heavenward
and standing there shifting from one oval of night to another.
Readings have come to take the place of genuine witness,
she said in her book, referring to the reflectors and signals of science
and how the finality of sense-data was the cue of a former epoch.
The week before I'd watched the clerk at the hardware store
hammer out my name a letter at a time on a brass tag for my dog
and as he neared the end I realized I was following his hand
letter by letter with the notion that he was pulling from an alphabet
that would spell me in a different way to the dream I had of myself.
But the final die, Y, came from between the X and Z I'd always
   known.
I didn't mean by *glamour* something in a magazine.
At its roots it draws on knowing and mystery circling within desire
like a system almost, but constant only in its moment,
a grammar of signs transformed and transforming.

I know the dreamer over the pool was not a genuine witness
or scientist of the first water, reading himself alone in the mediate
    thing.
And I know you weren't out there, pilgrim, with the mirror
horizontal in your hands, panning the oval waters like a fool,
but you understand: maybe something renewable in the skittering
    light,
maybe a likeness we could carry back across the street and call our
    own.

CHEESE

for William Harmon

1

One thing touches on another.

2

My youngest uncle usually smelled like cheese
until he discovered women.
The eyes and ears of the world
were all on war, but he was classified 4-F
owing to a broken back in his medical records
and couldn't go.
So he found himself among more women
than he could ever get around to
at the cheese plant where they all worked
for the war effort.
Before the women, he brought it home in loaves,
snugged under his jacket sleeves like dive bombs.
He told me how it was made
and how they weren't allowed
to eat any on the job.
We sat at night and ate the war cheese with saltines
until he started going out
with the women and wearing colognes.

3

Years later I was processing a compensation claim
for an insurance company I was working for.
A rural woman was claiming the cheese
at the plant where she worked
had infected her finger.
She said she had suffered with it long enough
and wanted money for her pain.
I recorded her testimony at the farm
where she lived alone with her mother,
but I was thinking the whole time of my uncle
and how different it had been at his cheese plant.
When I played back the tape later in the car
I could hear roosters in the background—
crowing for their cheese, I guess.

4

The other night at a college party
some students told me that eating cheese
is when you eat a woman.
I looked around at all the cheese in the room
and I thought of my uncle's wan smile:
more cheese than he ever dreamed
yet he wanted to be overseas.
I thought of the grown woman living at home
with her swollen finger, dreaming of money
for her pain from cheese.
I thought of the daughters in party linen,

pastels and fragrances so varied and fragile I'd never have
thought cheese on my own
or how it had to do with anything they wanted of life.
But there they were,
full and ripe as their mothers,
edible in the given figure,
though unaware of the overlap that brought them
into that moony congress in my mind, all of us duped
by this or that, our faces nonetheless
brightening with the word on our lips *cheese*
for any likeness, any touch of the future—
cheese, for whatever it means.

Easter Sunrise, the Constant Moon We Settled For

for Anne Gilland and Bland Simpson

All we knew was look low to the southeast,
but that was where the waning gibbous moon
and the one mercury vapor light on the island
had more or less taken over the horizon.
So we moved to another dune that at least
put the mercury vapor behind an eave
of the beach house being built next door.
The Atlantic hummed so steady in a strip of loose aluminum
in the half-done duct system that my son
joked how probably it was the workers still there.
They'd been drinking beer
all day Saturday and mixing country & western
with things like Jerry Lee Lewis
and Sting's new blue turtle album.
It isn't hard to figure how they'd believe most of that
more than the story of a carpenter
orbiting life and death
forever or how it would seem pointless
to make a sunrise service even of this comet
my son and I and our friend were trying to substantiate.
Finally we had to turn the telescope to the moon.
I don't know to this day if the only candidate
I could find for the comet was Deneb in Cygnus
or the tensed star in Sagittarius' shoulder
or simply Venus in the morning shuttle.
Or one of the others I read in a text.

Whichever, we couldn't hang enough of a tail on it
to offer as the once-in-a-lifetime gift
we'd promised our ladies drowsing on sofas inside.
We settled instead for the great Sea of Rains,
Mare Imbrium, one of the moon-man's eyes.
We settled for Tycho and its system of rays,
worn in another story as the Lady's Amulet.
We settled for the Rabbit's Head, our Ocean of Storms.
That was the story of things until dawn.
There were usually new shoes for me and my sisters on Easter.
Part of the myth was how my grandmother
used to shine my mother's black patents with a biscuit.
The man beyond the bridge to Swansboro that afternoon
came out of his trailer with a beer still in his hand
when his dog wouldn't stop barking.
We'd seen the FOR SALE sign
from the car and thought how desuetude
such as that inside and out of the house moldering
next to a trailer couldn't bring much more than twenty thousand
or so and we could maybe get a second mortgage
to fix it up for a tumbledown vacation lodge.
But the man said the deal included the nearmost lot
and rented trailer he'd been living in since the Air Force.
I saw he didn't want to have to leave the view:
when we asked if he knew the owner's price
he pointed to the Intracoastal
Waterway and the shuttle
of bright boats beyond his screened porch.
The way he said three hundred and fifteen thousand
told me it was all to him like light-years I can't understand
either or quite believe in, how one light
that reaches my eye was breaking from stone

the morning my mother's mother
was taking a biscuit from the oven
and another light tonight maybe having started out even
before Earth's sun was born.
Standing there beside the sign
I could count in my mind the channel markers
leading back up the Intracoastal to the inlet
that swept past our rented cottage on the island.
I could hear the strip of loose aluminum
over the distance that had hummed the whole weekend
to remind me somebody had the hard cash or easy credit
for this world. Listen, I had dreamed that last remaining lot
on the Point as mine more than once.
But I don't know what it would have taken to own the end
of an island any more than I know
where we thought we'd get twenty thousand
for Easter afternoon on the mainland.
I was thinking of the water and the light.
I've bought up whole coastlines that way, whole mountains.
So there we were—stargazers, comet seekers, workers boozed
and clocking overtime for strangers we never saw,
frontage owners, veterans in doublewides
with dogs hooked to clotheslines for news
they don't want to hear, one magnitude
after another of debt and credit and doubt—
and I thought of how sometimes it has to be enough
to settle for the moon, any music that matches the ellipse
of our lives.
I thought of how sometimes we have
to settle for whatever view there is,
though what we believe is the water running clean
with the tide of light reappearing morning after morning.

The Weather Wizard's Cloud Book

to L.D.R., Jr.

Of the clouds your father
photographed, you must remember most
those that day in the drizzle
as you stepped down from the trolley
and found him with his camera cloaked
and angled toward that part of the firmament
he needed to fix and leave with us,
his own record of weather's quirky provenance.

And how the weather of your youth
must have turned suddenly gray and sodden
within you, this man your father,
hunched over in the middle of the street,
photographing the worthless sky—or the rain
itself for all she knew, the girl you'd brought home
to meet the family, to somehow impress,
there, O lost, on your arm, a rigid adolescent silence.

Last month I touched a stone
that Thomas Wolfe's father had worked
into a doorstop for his bride-to-be.
J. E. W. FROM W. O. W. 1884
was all it said, and we can read
into that the coming remoteness that drove them
to Dixieland, by which I mean her literally
to her boardinghouse and Tom to the found door

of fiction. By which I mean too
you couldn't have known, there on the street
with your miserable teenage angst,
in what ways clouds were his meaning, likenesses struck
in black-and-white and Kodachrome for his book.
Nor could you have known your turning away was old hat
as sons go—sky, wet leaves and tarmac, red scarf all a book,
one book always a door to another, our story of loss never lost.

Cottonmouth, Angus, Redwing

for James Dickey

I was the one afloat on a film
of metal, nearly motionless in the pond
and thinking mine was the only language
in the riddle of three creatures
that had come to the water in unison.
I know that even with the paddle and fly rod
stock-still I was an array of heat and sound
signals across the water—and a reckoned symbol
constant in the eye of the cottonmouth
that slipped from a copse of willows
and swam to the facing shore in an unbroken succession of S's,
but the seeming heedlessness,
the no-need-to-talk-to-me, the fix of direction,
put me to thinking of the phylum
and our possible distinction—man, the thinking animal—
as though I were a sophomore again.
If the lowing of the Aberdeen Angus bull
brought the rest of the clan down the hill,
what was that syntax finally but an ecclesiastic set
of testicles so pendulous they swayed like something rung?
Not even the red-winged blackbird would signal anything more
than the silent semaphore of sex,
a quick dark blur coming at me and then its flash of red,
its veering spaceward.
I've since read that they know more than we think,
how a cat's spitting hiss, for instance,
is maybe mimicry playing on the world's fear of snakes.

So we could say the sorting out in the reptilian center,
the bellowing, the vaunted sexual plumage,
and what the Audubon Guide calls
a "gurgling, liquid *conk-kar-ree,* running up the scale
and ending in a trill,"
is all a kind of red-winged cotton-mouthed Angus language.
I think of how it veered and was gone,
and now I see myself alone—
the one differently verbed,
the one with time on my hands,
stopping to wonder, to remember a woman loved
and lost because we were not what we said.
Then I began again to put barbs
flying in the air,
none of them a part of my body.

Mountains by Moonlight

The postcard artist Harry Martin
could have gone to Mars
and not found a better full moon
for his Mountains by Moonlight.
It looks like a photograph
that's been hand-tinted and stars added.
When they were young
our grandparents sent it home
wishing everyone was there in the space
for writing messages.
The matte finish softens the moonlight
to where it's almost melancholy.
We don't know whether to lie down
and embrace our aloneness together on Earth
or fly to the moon.
It's pure nature,
not a Model T or AAA sign in sight,
but we know that outside the frame
the technology's in place for flight,
organ transplants, just about anything
you could imagine.
We know that beyond the mountains by moonlight
there is an architecture
our grandparents had to leave finally
in the same way they left these mountains.
We know that when we draw arrows,
as they did, to hotel windows
it's both to separate ourselves
from the sheer sameness of things *my room
was here* and yet double the evidence

we were part of that sameness
my room was there.
Once for a magazine article
I located Scott Fitzgerald's room
at the Grove Park Inn in Asheville
by standing in the parking lot
and counting up to the window
he had x'd on a postcard.
From the terrace he could see
the lights of Highland Hospital
where Zelda thought she was talking
to Christ and William the Conqueror and Mary Stuart.
Not even the mountains by moonlight
could put him to sleep,
so he took Luminal and Amytal
and a young married woman from Memphis.
Two years later he was in Hollywood.
We don't know if it was silliness
or loneliness that prompted the postcard
he sent to himself at the Garden of Allah
where he had rooms.
When they came home they brought us honey
in small jars shaped like bears,
assembly-line tom-toms with rubber heads,
cities we could shake into blizzards.
They asked if we got the cards.
Next year it would be palm trees
and a crescent moon.
We couldn't imagine them under those moons
with anything other than hearts
lifting to the broadened horizon.
We couldn't imagine them as having ever doubted
the light as they found it.

Night Fires

for Beth

I

If it's true that we don't know
our own hearts, or that we're rarely talking
about what we think we're talking about,
or that there're always at least two others
under the covers with us,
then we might just as well believe
that each of the simple moments we've tried
to hold for our lives
is its complex opposite, or close.
In which case the lamp's new mantle
in its first converting blaze from silk
to ash filament carried instead of our wonder
the final neural failure of bluefish
on ice in the Igloo cooler,
and we ate those fish in lemon and sweet butter
with a mind to the world's loss.
Likewise we should try to forget
the tiny lights
of Emerald Isle and Salter Path
blinking dreamily across the inlet and playing
in the mesh window of our tent.
No, each of those motions took hold
of time on a simple plane,
gathering with them the clean curves of our small boat
Spoondrift, anchored long-line and lifting

high-bowed in the blue-green tide,
the bunted clouds, the elderly kite collector's
mylar and nylon and rice paper
from all over the world, the dragons and streamers
he looped the whole weekend like carnivals.
Our tent was a comic feather
in the sea wind
until we staked it deeper,
laughing and stumbling in the dark.
And then we zipped ourselves in,
high on that dune with our little window to the water.

II

But I'm thinking too about how children want
to be over the deepest part.
As the house gets louder with bourbon
and basting the holiday venison at midnight
they skate alone with a cousin
on the pond that was slush at noon,
pressing closer to the center with each sweep.
It's that moment I have in mind,
neared by simple arcs,
but without the fatal prospect,
if that's possible.
I think of the night
on the North Yorkshire moor far from town
when we came upon the glowing
that looked first like a cavern
within which the deepening earth was on fire.
The next morning we found the great fallen tree

whose center even still was a far chamber
of embers for no reason we could understand.
If it had been a lake the night before
that did not burn us
we would have skated farther and farther out.

GIFTS DIVIDED

This morning the light lay across the table
in a way that lifted
from the shallow of a favored bowl the tincture
of petals I floated there

half without a plan over the course of a year
I had hoped long lost.
A simple fingerbreadth of water
would have buoyed—for what while longer?—

the corollas and separated petals
I'd brought to the table by fits and starts
to add to the light, but someone else
had always seemed to want

to see to that, so no sooner
than I'd floated them there I'd forgotten,
the registers of color
leaching each time to the cracked glaze

in the evaporation and ultimate press of nights
and days without replenishment.
I don't know how any of us could have thought parting
would rhyme with anything for a long time to come

except the obsessive sad riddle of sorting out
the blame for the failure of early happiness
and lightheartedness and all the other.
I'm not confusing the two kingdoms, the green one

wherein light is transformed into what I imagine
as always a kind of sweetness;
the other, ours,
unrooted except in an ongoing patter and patterning

I think of finally as elemental
translation in the neural fiber whose beauty
is in the embrace it tries to keep with the vanishing world.
Besides impatiens there were African violets,

a crocus or two, maybe one month an anemone.
There's a name for the system of finely cracked glaze
that carries these vague petal shapes
in fuchsia, faded purple, magenta—and it isn't memory.

It's what's left
when even that has done with its constant work of forgetting.

An Ideal of Itself

Sometimes laughter moved through the field
of feeling between us
in a way that made any notion but happiness
seem impossible. Not that we were stoned

or careless—just that we had been circled
from the start by a shared medium
the craziness and goodness
of the world could be filtered through.

We could ride with the top down
and the manic outpatients
trying to stroll
as a community of believers

along the sidewalk in their prescribed happy plaids
and fresh lithium couldn't have been funnier
for all the heartache in Alabama.
Say what you want to, we didn't laugh out loud

at them or the Greek restaurant
owner's oversized painting of the Acropolis in purples
and blues with philosophers lopsided
under clouds bearing their famous names like thought—

nor give anything less than his smile in kind
when he sent wine to the table
on our last night in his small town on the Chesapeake.
"For the young lovers," he said.

It's not that one way of reading
the world made up the tenor of our days and nights;
it all curves
in various arcs with the ongoing seasonal light.

Any mode of receiving the news of the moment alters
and is altered. Keats heard in the nightingale's voice
a full-throated ease transformed to plaintive anthem
within the course of a single song.

Even years later, though, when so little appeared
to be shared, there was still the middle-aged widow
from across the street, lost in time
and grief, asking on our doorstep to borrow

a birth control pill for a vacation with her new boyfriend.
And so always there's the sad thing with its tiny window
of negotiable hope. The noseless three-fingered politician
on local TV who was burned in the war:

when he jumped extempore
into a four-point speech with a finger for each point,
there wasn't a doubt about how to face the moment together.
Some of what Santayana says of the beautiful   .
comes to mind, a passage about its fulfilling a condition
in which there is no inward standard at odds
with the outward fact. In the way, say, light might rhyme
with an ideal of itself,

for good or ill, how Yeats cried and trembled
and rocked to and fro / Riddled with light

from the cold heaven that curved him unreasonably one day
into the blame of years past and aloneness,

its quantum his being
for the moment. I know there's a question
of what kind of witness to bear, what calls
on the past to make, what rhyming;

and I know that in sounding the memory we've made of feeling,
not everything is told in these extremes.
More and more often all I remember
is this or that landscape we passed through on our way somewhere.

❧ from *Said There Was Somebody Talking to Him Through the Air Conditioner*

Said There Was Somebody Talking to Him Through the Air Conditioner

for Barry Hannah

1

There is always one fiction or another trying to trade for real skin and
    bone,
just to turn around and drive that taken character back over
the border into phenomena with the story everywhere around him
    alive.
The charge is to claim whatever needs to be freed from fact: road,
    ruin, stretch of river
known by heart, ring or pendant, torn flag, fist in the face, ticket stub,
family plot, love and grief so riddled one with the other there isn't
    even a choice.
The character he's become says he doesn't want to die, but he's got
    only one foot in the fiction,
everlasting, the other in the grave of this life. And he needs us
    conscripted alongside him.
The night I was making my way back to the old stars and bars
    magnolias, for instance,
just after turning off the hard road: the man beside the bankrupt
    crossroads store
wanted to put his story against my ear like a cap pistol I couldn't quite
    tell from the real thing.
He thought when he flagged me down that they really were over
    there,
three niggers and a woman with a gun he said were trying to break in
    his trailer
and kill him, the character he had been traded for.

It was textured true enough in the crack of open window I gave him
to hold me idling there with the woven thing of race, gender, hair
     trigger.
The story, though, plotted or not, has to follow out that stranded line
     and make it come true.
I know, I have tried to tell some stories and when he said they were
     going to kill him
I thought now how did he get out here to the road to wait beside
     Doty's store
if they're trying to break in his mobile home that's too small for more
than one door and within earshot of where he's standing?
But he had already forced the five of them—the traded character he
     had become,
the three black men, a starved white woman I would guess—along
     with a gun
through the thin passage and into the Volvo with me and my sleeping
     sons,
what is woven through my life like no fiction I could ever work on
     the loom of days
and nights left in this world. And let me tell you, old pilot
of the silent craft, I could not be sure.
I could not be sure if by my promise to bring help I was leaving a man
to be shot at the side of a gravel road or getting distance on a sickness
     whose fiction
could turn and align my sons and me with those figures triggering
     loss
as though there were no other word for them.
There was cotton on one side of the road and soybeans on the other,
     the bean field broken
by a creek running down from the hill where my sister Donna had
     left the light on for us.
You've winged home yearly enough to know the time and place.

It has a texture and our lives gain whatever is gathered in the separate strands.

I'd driven a day and a half from Carolina, breaking the trip with a stop

at the Knoxville World's Fair, *the one about solar* the man at the Holiday Inn called it.

I wanted my sons to believe the taped lecture in the elevator to the sun sphere,

something about all one people under the sun.

We could do that and still joke at lunch in the Japanese pavilion

about how the soy sauce for the teriyaki was probably from Donna and Danny's last soybean crop.

The fireworks the night before broke out in a finale of red, white, and blue

flagging the river running through Knoxville and they played good old Sousa on the sound system.

The man beside my car late at night wanted me to stand beside him in the only country he could imagine.

2

My father, talking to a friend and thinking I was asleep, said it seemed slow but happened in a flash.

He said he aimed first for the rising sun in the middle of the fuselage.

He said he followed the smoke of his tracers and found the target and worked a line to the cockpit.

He said he could see the holes one after the other until the pilot, in propaganda-cartoon scarf

and leather helmet, turned and looked at him just before the cockpit window spider-webbed.

He said he and some buddies were frying eggs when they heard the plane come whining in

to use the island as backdrop for a long low run toward the *New Jersey*
out in the bay.

He said the pilot was zeroed-in on the battleship but strafing men and
tents along its path.

My father ran across open space to get to a .50 caliber gun on an aerial
mount,

and I see bullets puffing the dust of his camp like war movies he could
walk out of and did.

My father said all this, it was not a fiction, the island was Okinawa,
the pilot turned

and looked at him, he could see his strange eyes he said, it was not a
fiction, the newsclipping

my infant sister Jackie chewed to a ball of gray pulp and made into
what's now a family joke,

death we can laugh at like it is a sauce come to us in a bottle with
strange characters we don't know beans about.

My father calls them Japs and must hate them still, though he watches
the Braves on a Sony.

3

Jess Sutton in the room next to my father's at the nursing home

told me that Negroes have changed the game of baseball, I don't
know how,

but he could hardly bear what he saw when he came over to share the
Sony.

I tried to move him to stories of the timber he and my grandfather cut
when they were clearing

Yokna Bottom, hoping I'd get some whiff of Faulkner, but all he
would say was

That Bill he was a smart man and start back in on blacks.

Plus I couldn't be entirely sure he wasn't sometimes thinking of a
  Faulkner

who owned a peach orchard near the old hunting grounds.

According to my father, Jess was seeing snakes in the weeks before he
  died.

I know the texture here is beginning to read like the worn rag of race
  and guilt

but I can't say that Jess's feelings for blacks made him see snakes at the
  end of life.

He once told me stories that were free of hate and held me rapt for
  hours on end,

as true as the grain of ash and hickory felled and shipped from my
  grandfather's mill

to Louisville Slugger lathes, oak and cherry, walnut unscrolled in
  Memphis for veneer,

cypress, tulip poplar, plain or fancy, you name it they cut it, waded
  sloughs

and hacked briars to get to wood backlogged for boats, common
  doors, the kind of parquetry

that Jess got down on his hands and knees to see near Argonne in wonder

only three days before mustard gas just about blistered him out of his
  senses.

You'd think the latter would have given him characters and creatures
  enough to fill any fiction,

all he needed to bring back over to help free the facts of loss, but what
  doesn't get mixed

or turned tell me if you can, not forgetting the tricks and turns on
  both sides of the border?

My father came home from war with only a few shards of shrapnel
  for reminders

yet was left in a wheelchair for life by an ordinary accident in the
    Everglades
where he was clearing a swamp to sell to exiled Cubans for raising
    sugarcane.
The ever-smiling Bahamian I worked with there one summer called
    the cookies we shared *sweet biscuits*
and sent money back for his wife's fare to Florida, but it turned out
    she didn't want to come.
How answer love, or know what to any one person is sweet in the
    world? I'd count it such
in the end just to recall something like the peach orchard I saw in
    bloom one spring from a hillside,
or casting for blues with my father on Sundays where the St. Lucie
    feeds into the sea.
As though I'd written my own book, free of the strands that coil back
    through dream into silence.

4

Doty told us later that the man had come to his room in back of the
    store the previous evening
and said there was somebody talking to him through the air
    conditioner.
Doty let him in for the night.
In a pause in our talk of cotton and beans and needing rain, Doty
    looked out to the creek
where deputies were shining lights for *three niggers and a woman with
    a gun*
and said like somebody in local color fiction *They ain't nobody out
    there in that field.*

5

I think of this country, rhythms and idioms like that: Doty waiting for
    the brief lull
to let us know there was no one in the field to fear and his way of
    saying it, *they* for *there.*
I think of the mixed texture of belief, how the measures of voices and
    motions register
and randomly become a way we think of ourselves, our time and
    place, how in the same breath
with that lull and Doty's words I could name billboards, Booth and
    Koren cartoons, Bugs Bunny;
I could name the copy of *Tom Sawyer* in gray slipcase my uncle sent
    from Marshall Field's, Roosevelt
and the Kennedy voices, Nixon, King; I could name the homogenous
    voice chosen for the elevator tape
unreeling a future we could dream for children, or Brando's funny
    fleering desperado lines
in *One-Eyed Jacks* and Ben Johnson getting edgier and edgier in the
    Mexican fishing camp
they're holed up in until Rio can get his gun hand back; I could name
    Nicholson sweeping the table clean
in *Five Easy Pieces* after arguing with the waitress about toast for his
    chicken salad sandwich I think it was,
or my two favorite aunts in Memphis joking they'll pay in Yankee
    dimes for my chores,
or any of the voices and motions bidding from both sides of the
    border to be what we believe.
I think of how the voice that had been dubbed in when I saw Brigitte
    Bardot's breasts

was Hollywood French-accent and way out of sync, making the
  breasts, the first I'd seen moving on film,
even more isolate and without a history.
But I didn't object to any of it at the time, so dumb was my own
  chronicle,
and I could have come back over the border, I guess, if the loss in my
  life had run deep enough,
believing I kissed those breasts and not my aunts' faces, Met and
  Lydia.
I remember a day long ago the wind was in the pines and I was free to
  walk with a woman I loved.
The dried thistle she put in my buttonhole was the gray of a soft wool
  you'd reach out and touch;
still and all, I did not know where we were going.
Sometimes simply her profile blurred all loss for me, other times there
  was the rage
of a scene: her in an embrace I couldn't tell from fiction, couldn't tell
  if it was five summers ago,
yesterday, next year, couldn't tell if it was my private version of the
  broken-in mobile home,
the voice coming through the secondhand Whirlpool cooling the real
  room saying
the toast half-eaten on the plate before me is poison and everything
  else in the world.
The couple in the apartment above my uncle in Chicago wrapped
  aluminum foil
around their legs and feet to ward off the rays that he and the CIA
  were beaming at them.
Television correspondents in Alabama are standing by to film a man
  who called in
to say he's any minute now going to set himself on fire somebody hurt
  him so.

100

I don't know if the correspondents see him as another burning car on
     "Dukes of Hazzard"
or a place in the long line of anchors and stringers waiting to break
     Watergate again.
I don't know if he thinks the flare of skin and bone on the screen is
     the only way to make real his pain.
I know you start hearing all the rhythms, mixing all the voices and
     motions, you're in trouble,
trying for your own embrace with history, with one person, with this
     promise-land,
with the wind that can go atomic out of the worn-out pines
down through your Volvo antenna where one man is firing into a
     playground in L.A.
and another is setting the new national record in a McDonald's in
     San Ysidro,
dropping Mexicans and Americans of all ages on the floor of his
     wrong fiction still clutching hamburgers.
On television his wife says it's the president's fault and it seems to her
     like being asleep
on the couch and waking up to a TV show, his mother left him at age
     eight and he lost his job.
He can't hear the elevator tape of all one people; he put on his
     aluminum boots and walked out.
He can't hear the plain talk of bankrupt Doty *they ain't nobody out
     there in that field.*
My young dog Moose, Shiloh's Golden Moose, was woozy and sick
     from motion,
not bad fiction, riding home out of the pines in the long foreign wagon.
Sometimes that kind of dog-level equation is the only way to figure
     things, where you know the answer,
dumb and sentimental, is solid ground for the little fellow and he
     doesn't have to worry

with the half-joke of history in his name or his buddy's, Stonewall
  Jackson Bear.
Other times all I know to do is laugh and tell stories, when the truth
  won't work,
when too many rhythms start jamming the instrument that otherwise
  tells if the signal is fictive.
I know the pilot meant to kill my father I could trust the motion that
  brought the thistle
to my buttonhole the pond at Shiloh was left a bloody mess walking
  home after the war
my mother's grandfather had to have stone bruises lanced along the
  way because he had come clean
out of his boots and that is no fiction my sister Donna left the light on
  for us my grandfather
had sawmills all over Yokna Bottom before he and Jess Sutton left
  they had found
a permanent place in the literature of the land you figure it out there
  were animals drawn
on the side of McDonough's Store with the names of hunters who had
  shot them bears and snakes and what
they called panthers the man heard voices talking to him there was
  something strange in his eyes
the cookies were sweet biscuits to Desmond like his woman made my
  aunts meant kisses when they said
Yankee dimes I drive a car from Sweden sometimes I do not know
  where we are going.

6

But let's say we've got them all in the cage for now—voices, snakes,
  x-ray waves, whatever.

Let's say they're with the diamondbacks my grandfather would put in
   burlap bags and take to Overton Zoo.
And that all the way to Memphis I could hear them buzzing in the
   trunk of the old green Ford.
Say too that after his donation was recorded at the herpetarium we
   would go the Peabody Hotel
to drink coffee and cokes and joke with his friends from the Southern
   Lumbermen's Association
about the ducks waddling to the fountain in the lobby and I could
   forget the snakes.
Maybe nobody but me knows if that's fiction or autobiography or
   something in between,
but right now what's important is the story has given us a way of
   containing things and continuing:
the snakes are in the cage with the mix of fictions we've named and
   not loose in the floor of the old Ford
like one was once and we know which is which.
That's important because the no less than life and death question we
   could pose here
would take a clear mind, no Mr. Snake-Eyes whispering through the
   Whirlpool,
no sentimental stories of grandfathers tipping doormen to get duck
   eggs for grandsons
to take back to Mississippi and how I raised a flock starting with that
   incubated egg.
That is, looking at it without tears or coils in our eyes, do we say the
   man's crossroads fiction had a gun
pointed at him because he must have wanted deep down to die, and
   do we say by the same thanatotic token
there are some walking dreamers who'd take the missionary position
   to mean it's not for life we love
and would with purpose suffer us all into what the doctor from
   Vienna once characterized as the peace of the inorganic?

Or do we say the mind's various displacements and translations don't
    allow the grand answer?
Maybe it's one thing to be in aluminum foil overalls at the crossroads,
your handkerchief of loss in somebody's highbeams,
and another to be telling a story with something like a master race in
    mind
to the point of trying to turn brown eyes to blue with hypodermic dye
    or V-2s, and even another to believe
the little kamikaze fiction called *Floating Chrysanthemums* that makes
    a heaven
of the run to Okinawa behind the fighter escort my father is going to
    set his sights on.
Because if all of that and the fact of installing rattlers in the ruptured
    trunk of an old Ford
point to the same desired embrace I've got to forget how he and
    others I remember
seemed to love life and laughter to where you'd believe their charity.
My fourteen-year-old son told me the other day when we were
    talking about a science fiction movie
that he wouldn't too much mind going back to the Fifties to live
    because rock and roll would be new
and there wouldn't be the arms race to worry about and other things.
To turn it around I guess I'd have to get in a time machine movie and
    be fourteen in the Eighties.
For one thing, I'd want to know how often the time fused to my wrist
    would flash on me like that watch
from Hiroshima on the magazine cover the week he and I talked
    about music and time and the movie.
For another, I'd want to know how strong I believed the frail simple
    thing we let it rest on:
how you have to live in your own time and believe in the best people
    you can find.

It wasn't deathless prose by any stretch but I did think of that passage
    about only the names
of things having dignity and I tried not to embarrass us with too
    many things that didn't have names.
Nor did I want to get too confessional for comfort, about how most of
    my friends and I
at one time or another in the not too golden past would have taken a
    ticket to the Fifties in a flash,
though more for a different chance at love and clarity.
There's always another story that can be made of loss even if we're
    dead-set on losing the likeness as well,
and I'm not saying we are: I don't know what it means that a fair
    number of us can trace
the sad and paradramatic fact of near neural ruin to both the changed
    prospect of days and nights
remaining to make good and plots that now seem scripted to the
    notion there's nothing worth another chance.
Saying that, I see how easily it shifts from the private text, where I
    thought it had its only bearing,
to the common one weighing on my son.
I don't know when worry begins to go beyond tending a flock of
    ducks
to trying to name and place love and work and death in a story that
    has a future.
At my son's age I was barely free of Little Moron jokes, one of which
    comes to me now with a timing
I guess it's best to laugh at: the one about Little Moron throwing the
    clock out the window
because he wanted to see time fly. Little Moron wanted to see time fly,
    old pilot.
And all this time I'm trying to think how even the simplest among us
    wants

a story that frees the body from the fact of itself, its own moment.

I am half blind, so to speak, and probably going deaf, a ringing in my
ears only white noise will block.

The doctors cite time's famous flight, gunshot, chainsaws, rock concerts.

Once I was so close to the amps I could see the gray in Garcia's beard

and they jacked up "Johnny B. Goode" to where I couldn't hear
anything but the Dead for days.

Your dead electric hero Jimi Hendrix played it another way, same
lyrics—leader of a big old band,

country boy from way back up in the woods among the evergreens,
maybe someday his name in lights—

but different texture, the tight braiding he made of the story and his
own life.

There was a voice loosed in the man's head that night that wouldn't
yield.

He wanted me to bring the white noise over the line to him.

He wanted me and my sons to cross over with his story around us alive.

7

Once a voice separated itself from a graduation party in the yard
below me and I knew

without having met him he was the father of the friend we were
celebrating.

I saw him only that once, which was also the last time I celebrated
anything with my friend.

It was the pitch and timbre of place telling me who he was, the
resonance of landscape known in the light

of seasons, a cadence falling always homeward, away from how my
friend must have pitched and tumbled

to the small crater that opened for him over a land mine the next
spring somewhere in Vietnam.

I took the voice coming to me through the open window on the glass
     porch where I was tying my bright tie
back down to the party and my friend's father was the substance of it.

8

For two winters on their nights with me my sons slept beneath the
     pelts of whitetail deer.
Probably it started with the open sleeping bags they chose for
     bedcover, the memory of our voices
within rings thrown by fires of driftwood or downed trees; from there
     it was only natural
to take the pelt from the foot of the bed and layer it between body and
     down bag.
They took turns with the North Face bag we once spread for a meteor
     shower years ago,
the night I began the story about a cat whose tail caught fire from a
     falling star
and how it was saved: *The Cat That Wouldn't Scat, the Ball That
     Wouldn't Fall, the Car That Wouldn't Go Far, and the Clown Who
     Brought Them All Around.*
Long title.
If it seems skewed and inconsistent that we'd work so hard to save
     the cat
and then turn around to hunting deer and doves and such a few
     seasons down the road,
both here in Carolina and on the old hunting grounds only miles from
     Doty's,
I don't want you trying to tell me why if you're wearing the fancy
     boots or some flashy coat of skins.
I guess if you believed to the point of weaving your own belt out of
     hemp or synthetics

you could maybe talk from that techno-domestic principle to a kind
   of holiness

I can't imagine right now—not having the story you'd need to tell.

Listen, we ate the flesh, we saved the pelts, if there's a bone left in the
   dog-yard it's fossil.

Call it whatever you like, but we are trying for a story that will bind
   the years, follow out the stranded lines

of our first dreams, some of it a texture we can touch and tell.

If this part of the telling cancels out our story for anyone I care about,
   I'd say again that we watched

the night sky for its fire, we freed the ball suspended—it seemed
   forever—beyond the boy's open hands,

we walked the dogs.

It's a long story, parts of it as worn and gray as hooves, old roads,
   photos we keep in an album

for the sake of sentimental history, the news chewed to a pulp.

I do not know where it is going.

There was a time the meteors and seasons fell with a sadness I did not
   want my sons to see,

the gray filtering to their mother's eyes and mine as we failed.

Part of a story is how it is told in another, that reach of the voice with
   ways to imagine.

I knew to trust the motion bringing the thistle to my buttonhole.

If I didn't want them fully given to their own time, that somehow
   they could find a different constellation,

it's not like I meant the only dream is in the lost circles of sacrifice and
   elementary wonder.

One way I can believe the simple tape droning up to the top of a
   world's fair is how the sun comes slanting

into the fiction of itself, the gold sphere of one-way glass we are in,

and there is no way out for it but through our breath and eyes, the
   light translated and joining

what we will see and say at night by the crossroads store or in the
  letter
with money and maybe sweet biscuit crumbs or on the face of time
  held half-cocked at the open window
as though all laughter is mad. I looked in the man's eyes and could not
  tell.
But don't you see how they could hit on something else?
They could put the gun down and turn the old Whirlpool off.
They could go out by the water of the creek and wonder at the stars
  together.
And for a moment it would not matter where we are going, the voices
  gathering for the story to tell.

❦ from *Water Tables*

For Joshua, at His Great-Grandfather's Grave

Unimpressed by all that marks his passing—
words and a name
on the travertine wall, the days and years—
you turn your small face away
to where the trees breathe
a light song,
life from the mountains.

Somewhere in all this green or beyond
can the earth's skin be dying?

I watch stonemasons
lifting the same white marble
to face a near wall of empty vaults.
The foreman shows me blueprints
drawn at the Italian quarry.
One legend translates "all is marked."

Will the stream be clear
you put your knee beside?

The stone, of course—
marked in numbers we all can read.
And to that I add your forehead and mine,
your mother's here beside us,
her grandfather's marked in this marked stone,
it is all marked
and I accept
for us all.

I accept
that all is marked for this wall, this valley,
that this is what the numbers add up to,
I accept, I accept,
all but what has been marked against
your green assembly.

The smoke of what we have dug
from these mountains
hangs over every city
like a final trumpet.

Thieves strip off the blanket of topsoil
for the rich darkness that sleeps there.
They leave the slopes without cover
and when it rains, nothing holds.
Miners with black lung
drop into the shafts each morning,
knowing no other way.

Can you hear me?
I am trying to make it right
for when I am words and a name
on the wall, my days
and years all marked.

I am shouting over the walls for you
the message I have found in your looking away:
there is only one faith
and it is written in these leaves.

Naming the Moon

The moon is in the patch of trees on our hill
and so we go out to name and claim it
for the first time together.
No matter that in the window by your bed alone
it has been *airplane* or *car* or *light;*
tonight it is clearly *moon,*
as big and pale as your mother's belly twenty months ago,
though diminishing as it clears our hill
and pulls toward the Milky Way.   *Moon   Moon*
Your small butt stirs against my chest
and as the word takes hold of you like a possession
I sense tides beginning to draw again over fossil shells
in the limestone wall beneath your boots.
A mist like salt spray finds the light hairs
around my nostrils. I know these stars
were where the seas fell. Sand is running out
from under us.
Trying to hold you from the undertow,
yet steadily giving you to the moon,
I almost call out *airplane airplane car light.*
But then I hear your new word turn to *cold*
and realize it is November, not dead waters,
stirring us. We go inside,
you to your bath, I to a whirlpool of words
that become the whirlpool of draining water
you put your finger in to claim whatever is there.
And whatever it is
now as you come naked into my room bringing back to me

trees hill an airplane cowboy boots limestone dead seas a light
I remember it is out of my hands,
for finally, turning, you give me the moon
before I forget.

On the Way

This is the children's road.
No way to find it but with my sons.
The world is something else
when we get altitude.

Hard to see it otherwise
even when flying alone
on the pass they give me for the flight out.

We saw the dangers long ago
and found a song or a saying
to keep us free.

At the pound we say
every dog has his day.
It doesn't mean much but it gets us by.

The railroad crossing has a song *and* a saying.
You know the song
but this is the first time
the saying's found a page—
let the low side drag
we yell, looking both ways even on green.

If the sun finds an open blind
and shows us someone sleeping
we've got the right tongue to josh him with:
Frère Jacques, Frère Jacques,
dormez-vous, dormez-vous?

The best part's when we ring
all the bells on the hill.

After that there's the valley so low
you have to hang your head over
to hear the wind blow.
We get solemn on that one
but it doesn't last.

I think they already sense I'm the old cowboy
sentimental and silly to the end.
We learned a new one today
and here I'm still humming it on the solo run:
From this valley they say you are going,
I shall miss your bright eyes and your smile.

ON THE ISLAND

1

Things had not been right
and you thought another place
would bring you back around to your old self.
The horoscope said a journey
under the sign of Cancer.
The madman was waiting for you
at his small airstrip beside the Gulf.

2

And now on the island you are thinking
everything will fall back in place.
The madman is spraying the frozen moving parts
of all he owns with 3-in-1 oil:
his Shakespeare reel, the clasp on his tackle box,
the Amphi-Cat that will cart you to the edge
of the island where fish are feeding.
Things ought to go smooth
he says, shards of rust melting around him
like Baked Alaska.

3

The crabs watch you like a Greek play
they have seen repeatedly.

4

The surf curls with the tropes of your reel,
you are bailing line, working your lures
through the waves like a hairdresser.
Everything is going smooth
until the fish begin feasting on your baits,
striking whatever hook you throw
concealed in acrylic minnow-shine or colored feathers.
You forget the trained bones
of your wrist, the follow-through, the line's fine arc.
You throw your whole arm away
like soft-drink bottles.
You come to understand men
shooting buffalo
from the windows of trains.

5

Where you are becomes a train
the madman is conducting
and it trundles you and your gasping luggage
to night around the butane's blue eye
in his driftwood hotel.
The stubs of that trip in your hand,
soaked in Wild Turkey sours and fried fish,
you hear how the vacuum-cleaner salesman
brought his secretary to pure frenzy
with stag films on a motel wall.
The joke was the bellboy
eyeing the projector in its squat case.

Traveling light.
The haberdasher has one better than that:
the woman and the goat . . . Spanish fly in her drink . . .
Outside the crabs go wild as turkeys
and edge toward the waste heap at the door.

6

On the second day in the surf
the shark will take the blues away
from the stringer floating too close to your hip.
You think of your white poplin legs
strutting like a minstrel show in his aquarium,
how he can make a legless singing toy of you.
But do not fret—since he cannot dance
on your legs back into his twelve-part band
he is probably only after the one fish that knows
the celestial step, the shared part, of his sign;
your few remaining hours here belong to the fiddler,
the spider, perhaps a random limulus.
Their sign is now everywhere around you.

7

Distress has swooped a plane over the island
to bring the cannister with muslin flagging its fall.
Inside, a message for the madman:
COME AT ONCE
THE RIVER IS ON FIRE
ALL THROUGH YOUR CITY

MEASURES ARE BEING TAKEN
His only prospect a horizon dark with carbon,
he has flown off into the sunset
like a desperate measure of his own.

8

And now high tide makes a cut
through the thin island.
You cannot hear
what they are saying on the other side,
figures weaving in their own boozy moon,
bodies glistening with spindrift.
You hear only the collapse
of waves, the shark's parting song,
the rasp of crabs dancing on sand.
Soon they will be moving
all over your body,
burning you down
like the things of the earth
you could not live with.

ANOTHER SENTIMENTAL
JOURNEY

Time is a tease. Time is a tease—
because everything has to happen
in its own time.
      —Nadja

Here is something from the past this morning,
outside the raised shade,
something you suppose the wind has blown
up to the French doors of the bedroom.

It is a Time-Life disc
from an ad that came in the mail,
Sentimental Journey on one side,
blank on the other,
part of an offer that said there is more,
there is much much more.

If you could mend
where the dog's teeth broke through
before he dropped it at your door
(not the wind after all),
smooth the wrinkles,
and get just a snatch of what the past danced to,
wouldn't you order the whole package?

Isn't that enough—
a little teasing from Time?
You don't really want to reach out

in a past time, do you,
and find again that something
has come between your hand
and the flimsy curtain
you want to pull away?

THE BALLET OF HAPPINESS

A letter comes from the city today
where she has just gone,
my student of a year ago,
to study art.
She says it is a long story
and asks among other things
if I am happy.

Instead of an answer of my own to send back,
I think of what she once gave
to the same question: she said no, not much,
but went on to name what in recent memory
had made her happy:

It was friends calling in the moonlight
to her balcony, saying they had come
to dance for her The Ballet of Happiness.
Which they did, their bright mescaline eyes
smiling up at her, and when it was over
they bowed like children in a play
and left—just walked across the grass,
leaving her dazzled and happy
with the funny shapes of their footwork
fading in the dew.

I have carried that dance a year in my head,
not realizing until now that for us too
friends appear on the damp lawn
and give us their blurred version

of a story they want to live
where image arises from image, freely,
and their kind bodies move for the words.

And we can be happy
because they have not come to take anything
but our smile
which we give in the freest of associations,
for they may never come again
or else forget and stay too long.

So am I happy?
It is a long story
and my feet are moving into moonlight
like clouds; friends are waiting.

The New Rheostat

for Vereen & Jane

You are proud
you put it in with your own hands
and so I ask you
to show me your favorite setting.
Allowing for candles I have to imagine,
you turn it down.
This is how it will be
some evening soon:
there are no place cards;
we are free
to move in this illumination
as if the moment were unconditional.
It is like going to bed
and finding our old bodies,
the faces we wore in the caves,
the light the water dimmed.

What Lasts

for Gerald

"They'll be memories,"
he said of the pictures you'd just taken of us
and there was nothing we could add to that.
The simple man had said his simple truth.
Off Hatteras, we will remember years later,
seeing the prints, *out along the Gulf Stream
where the water is two colors.*
And so we could not tell him "nothing lasts"
or point to the dolphins
fading in the hold of our boat
or work aloud with what he had said
as though it were a passage in a text.
We could only nod and say he was right,
thinking to ourselves it was a good way
of keeping the idea simple: how these images
would develop into a history
the mind has amended to its own needs—
like your medley from the Fifties
or your story of having to kiss Big Arms
in the burnt-out casino
or stories of the trouble we've all had with *flux*—
thinking those things and smiling
as if for a moment in the play of light and water
we could believe there was no more to it than that.

THINK BACK

The hummingbird that tried to fly through the glass
of your big window last summer like a plane of light,
was it bringing you a promise?

How long can you hold out in that living room?

When you found the hummingbird, weren't ants working
the channels of its body like spiritual electricians
wiring the wing of a cathedral for miracles?

It All Comes Together Outside the Restroom in Hogansville

It was the hole for looking in
only I looked out
in daylight that broadened
as I brought my eye closer.
First there was a '55 Chevy
shaved and decked like old times
but waiting on high-jacker shocks.
Then a sign that said J. D. Hines Garage.
In J. D.'s door was an empty Plymouth
with the windows down and the radio on.
A black woman was singing in Detroit
in a voice that brushed against the face
like the scarf
turning up in the wrong suitcase
long ago after everything came to grief.
What was inside we can only imagine—
men I guess trying to figure what would make it
work again. Beyond them
beyond the cracked engine blocks and thrown pistons
beyond that failed restroom
etched with our acids beyond that American Oil Station
beyond the oil on the ground
the mobile homes all over Hogansville
beyond our longing
all Georgia was green.
I'd had two for the road
a cheap enough thrill

and I wanted to think
I could take only what aroused me.
The interstate to Atlanta was wide open.
I wanted a different life.
So did J. D. Hines. So did the voice on the radio.
So did the man or woman
who made the hole in the window.
The way it works is this:
we devote ourselves to an image
we can't live with and try to kill
anything that suggests it could be otherwise.

THE TREE MAN AT THE PARTHENON TOURIST HOME

Probably once a month
I see his truck of trees
parked overnight at the tourist home
and I wonder what brings him there.
Most of the big truckers
keep on trucking.
I want to think it has to do
with all the elephant ears,
not the replica of the Parthenon
down the street.
I want to see him one summer evening,
the tree man, sitting out on the porch
with the proprietress, dreaming
the one rain forest in Nashville.
But that can't be the only reason.
I called the lady and she said
she has to take them in
when the first frost falls.
And in the basement they die off
for the winter.
What about those bare months, tree man?
All your greenwood trees
are for the new rich in Chattanooga or Atlanta.
Is it that she's promised to take you down
to where the whole elephant walks,
and on into that secret graveyard
all the white hunters dream of?
Or are you trying, tree man,
to remember something forever?

The Motion of Bodies

I

Two bodies attracting each other
mutually describe similar figures
about their common centre of
gravity, and about each other mutually.
      —*Newton,* The Motion of
      Bodies, *Book I, Proposition 57,*
      Theorem 20

As two skaters are drawn out of their strangeness
to an open space on the ice,
so our bodies are drawn to this opening.
And as easily as the skaters move into descriptions
of, say, the common figure 8,
so we discover the figures
that mutually describe our correspondence,
each curve leading into another
more outrageous than the last.
Hard to resist the notion
that these figures have infinite possibilities,
the way we defy the gravity of this place.

II

If a rare medium consist of very
small quiescent particles of equal
magnitudes, and freely disposed at
equal distances from one another: to

find the resistance of a globe moving
uniformly forwards in this medium.
—*Book II, Proposition 35,*
Problem 7

Imagine the medium
consists of the small particles of my vision.
I cannot call them rare,
but toward the fine apparatus of your breasts
as you move uniformly forwards in this medium,
they are uncommonly quiescent and freely disposed.
Move deeper into the condition
and feel these particles of my seeing surround your body,
impinging enough to prove their equal magnitudes,
yet giving way enough to suggest
that our findings are close at hand:
the perfect resistances, the solid proof.

III

There is no oval figure whose area,
cut off by right lines at pleasure, can
be universally found by means of
equations of any number of finite
terms and dimensions.
—*Book I, Lemma 28*

These are the right lines at pleasure,
no question.

I'd even try to revive a worn figure
and say we're floating
in a balloon of our own design
but that would leave out too much—
the way your body's curves
confer with space, for instance,
in terms so elliptical
they've taken on the dimensions of mystery.
The best we can do
to avoid the possible clouds of suspicion
is press on, we sense, casting the lines
and tending the small flame
that holds us aloft.

IV

*All motion propagated through a
fluid diverges from a rectilinear progress
into the unmoved spaces.*
    —Book II, Proposition 42,
        Theorem 33

See yourself as the fluid medium
through which this motion is propagated.
We both are swimmers there,
I in you, and you in yourself with me.
Feel the progressions of our strokes
follow their given lines
until finally a motion in each of us breaks
and diverges into the unmoved spaces,

the still water that waits like a sky
for the crescents ringing our bodies.

V

> *To find the distances of the pulses.*
> *—Book II, Proposition 50,*
> *Problem 12*

We'd have to find time and space.
As a rule, I can count on my hands
but right now they're tuned
to the quartz crystals strumming in your body,
the only timepiece they trust.
So don't move, let everything
take its own good time.

NATURAL GROWTH

Plant your eyes in the solid bank of trees,
in the room where the pines are counting their long green.
Let your vision grow into the other kingdom.
Look at it this way:
if cows come
grass is happy to be straw
in the mortar that holds the meadow together.
Poppies support their habits
through only the most benevolent of aggressions.
The willow on the river's eroding ledge
says *no money in the bank*
but still it joins its family in green huzzas
for light and space.
That's when you can tell
if your eyes have taken root:
every cheer that reaches you is one
you know by heart.

Family Business

Same provisions season after season,
nothing fancy. But they keep the doors open
even after the others have rolled in
their awnings and gone to the islands.
The plain sign beaming in the snow
satisfaction guaranteed
evergreen   evergreen

A Question of the Elements

"Help me keep my powder dry,"
I pled with the flood, "I'll back your cause."
"Can't play favorites," it whispered,
"stand tall, you'll get the word: *river on the rise.*"

I tuned in the lightning,
asked, "What's safe ground?"
"Stay low," was all it said,
"I'll give you the sign."

I wired the wind for hints or charts;
answer came 4th-class mail:
"I play the earth's curve, sweetheart,
you plot it."

Finally there is nowhere to turn but earth,
crying, "I'm yours."
"You can count on me," it yawns,
"would I let you down?"

The Green World

Move through it
as though it were a house whose windows
your breath has been floating
in and out of from birth.

The attic of course is full
of the essential stuff—the wedding veil,
an old box camera, watercolors, the winning thesis.
Whatever we thought was worn out.

In the root cellar
is the food we will need for the winter.
There's wine down there too.
Drive you out of your head.

Sorry we forgot to mark the years
on the bottles. Some are better than others,
but there's no way
you can be sure.

We'll watch for you
to come reeling up the stairwell.
Just don't knock over the lantern
or wake up the children.

The best view's from the verandah.
Always a spare chair or two.
Birds chirp, dogs bark.
You can see the bend of the river.

Make yourself at home.

ONE OF THE BIG DIFFERENCES

I slept with a girl steady once
who stole water glasses from the grill—
two or three a week in her purse,
each one dumb with its lip dream.
The last kiss, though, was for the brick wall
bracing itself behind the oilman's dorm.
I was dumb too in my own caul of thirst:
when the moon pulled her down one dark month
with the lost water, she broke us all
out of our vows, the identical O's,
a man's name on every one and mine the last
echoing that she bled and we couldn't care.
Cut yourself to ribbons
getting out of that girl's hair.

Patching Up the Past with Water

1

For a beginning
let yourself be drawn like debris
to all the great bodies of water;
I will be there
asking you to help
lift up a hand of water
and reach into a time
we dream to change.
No matter that even before
your first palm is taken away
the water washes off itself
like quicksilver off a wall of glass
or that your hand becomes a broken colander
wired loosely to the wrist,
sieving whatever drifts by,
no matter—we also want to keep an eye peeled
for anything that might give the past away:
bits and pieces, twigs and such.
We can begin anywhere
you find an entry.

2

It could be a key
from the Hotel Pemaquid

where the room keys have all been lost
over the years.
For ventilation, the desk clerk will say,
just leave the door ajar
and pull the door curtain for privacy,
nothing has ever been stolen.
Find the room matching your secret key,
lock yourself in and ponder
the clutter of your uninsurable goods,
the fog that curtains
the Maine coast by morning.
Listen as confusion sweeps up the maid service
when they arrive at your door screaming
nothing has ever been stolen, there is someone
needing to trust you
in every room on the hall.
You see your door as *out there*
and fumble to unlock it
through the drape of fog.
The dead air, the foggy misapprehension, the unimaginable
water.
Anything to help you understand
this history better.

3

A song maybe
but nothing resembling this stone shore.
Someone in lime-green half-sleeves
knows the words. South of here.
The instruments are in fake alligator cases

piled near the lake in the grass,
and he is stretching his arms
toward the one he can chord for this song,
seeing us walk the line
off the interstate.
His band, blowing smoke over the lake
and waiting for the Plymouth to cool down
to their chill lime shirts,
will hear the song come off the water,
bluegrass,
and give him the rest of the music
his words need.
They forget the VFW dance three hundred miles away—
these are the old words
they can't leave alone,
broke with love again and singing.
We know now that peace won't come
the whole night through.

4

A dream drifts by, one that recurs:
the bride your wife once was
is the one Mayans dress in precious metals
and stones for the sacrificial lake.
And now a guided tour back by steamer
to the waterfall above her pool:
you, your miserable guide,
the deserted concession stand.
But the dream changes; in this one
you are alone.

In the water the riches you have been coming for
are nothing but silt
except for eyes brighter than any fire,
reaching you like hands.
Whatever the old ritual denied
has been yours for the taking all along.

5

If the rain comes
let it take you back.
What was it your father brought you
in his voice out of the rain?
You breathed your question alone in the rear seat
that night in the middle of the field
when he came back to the car with your youngest uncle
and the sack of frogs from another man's pond.
The brief interior light
from the opened door in his face
gave you that question and part of its answer;
his changed voice told you more:
the man whose sounds were lost in the dark rain
had caught them at his pond's edge.
That much was available at the border
of their words in the car
as they tried to talk away from you,
but you would never know the secret of their tremor.
Now in the rain
you ask your father to take you back,
show you where the man came out of the trees
down to his pond,

say what was said and done,
not to turn away.

6

For long spells at a time
any leaf we turn over
turns out to be the chemical paper
where a Polaroid picture cleared
and was torn away.
We trace the shadows of its slate gravestone
as though we were doing a temple rubbing,
and always the ghost of a woman
emerges in silver at the water's edge.
Three frames away, a white heron
in flight, the same day, the same water.
That's when the tracings in our hands
take flight or else become a montage
of all the wrong that lovers always do.
Nothing we can do but return
to where our decoys are waiting in their dream
and there resume whittling at the worn reed of desire
that calls up time after time
from its wooden throat
enough down here for us both.

7

Eventually this intimation:
some matters water won't solve.
Her divorce was four years ago.

Here are new friends, white wine on ice,
and the cigarette coming back around from hand to hand
on this Saturday afternoon where Leaf River eases south
out of a little town in Mississippi called Petal.
She had to get free. You can understand:
he was the one who hung the gaudy dress in her closet.
Leaf and petal she is thinking
wash it all away but leaf and petal.
But still his image flashes up
with its one lesson: *root and stalk.*
And water won't tell why.

8

Children hear what water tells best of all.
It calls up to them from the river
walk out of the empty mansion on the bluff
and find the sundial in the garden.
The line looped around its pedestal
will lead you down the hill to the white boat.
Cut it loose and let it drift away.
Be free of the death they planned for you.
It wasn't malice; they painted the boat each summer
and remembered the customary favors.
Wave your love up the slope to them
and ease into the water.
Follow your death only as far as you have to.

9

So much in our mothers' eyes
we could not help.

I think of a photograph
of my own mother at seventeen.
She is kneeling beside a lily pond
in someone's yard.
The bathing suit is a one-piece wool jersey
and her body is almost as white as the clouds.
No man has seen it all.
There are goldfish in the water
her hand is in,
but we cannot see them.
Now she has lifted her face to the camera
and I am wishing we could be true—
my father, my sisters,
you and I, all of us
waiting out here in the future
like the stone frog her other hand rests on.

10

Somewhere your hand or mine
will come to rest
on the water table bearing only itself,
the true food of this dream.
In it we taste fossils, clouds, failure.
For all our palms of water, our sieving,
this is what we come to,
a water that offers nothing
from the private past,
water that down to its last
and smallest particle resists our will.
As it begins to move through us

we feel its secret in each lapse
of our pulse *no one moment separate from another*
no one motion
Never that dreamed absence of succession
in which to reassemble the whole being.
And yet our hands are straining
as though some image, free and alterable,
had dropped from the table
and lay within reach.

❦ From *Let Not Your Hart*

Grabbling in Yokna Bottom

The hungry come in a dry time
To muddy the water of this swamp river
And take in nets what fish or eel
Break surface to suck at this world's air.

But colder blood backs into the water's wood—
Gills the silt rather than rise to light—
And who would eat that meat
Must grabble in the hollows of underwater stumps and roots,

Must cram his arm and hand beneath the scum
And go by touch where eye cannot reach,
Must seize and bring to light
What scale or slime is touched—

Must in that instant—on touch—
Without question or reckoning
Grab up what wraps itself cold-blooded
Around flesh or flails the water to froth,

Or else feel the fish slip by,
Or learn that the loggerhead's jaw is thunder-deaf,
Or that the cottonmouth's fangs burn like heated needles
Even underwater.

The well-fed do not wade this low river.

No Man's Good Bull

No man's good bull grazes wet clover
And leaves the pasture as he came.
My uncle's prize Angus was bloated
And breathing hard by afternoon
On the day he got into our clover pasture
Before the sun could burn the dew away.
He bellowed death from the field
As we grappled to hold his legs and head;
Our vet inserted a trocar between his ribs,
             let the whelming gas escape,
And to show us the nature of that gas
Put a match to the valve . . . a blue flame caught
         and the animal bolted from us,
Heading into the woods along the river bottom,
Turning only to test the new fire
             of his black side.

Each night we see his flame, blue and soft
                beside the river,
As he steals in before dawn
To plunge his head into wet clover,
Graze his fill,
      blaze up,
And answer that which lows to him in heat.
We watch him burn—
         hoof, hide, and bone.

Turtles from the Sea

Cradling all that was not edible
The scooped-out shell lay steaming
In an empty field of sugarcane
Where we had dumped it after bringing

Turtles from the sea, dividing them
Among ourselves and dressing each
Ancient hulk in stealth for fear the law
Had seen and tracked us from the beach.

Cast-off vital parts grew black, then green,
And simmered in the Florida heat.
Buzzards circled, swooped, and took what parts
The dogs or wildcats would not eat.

Fang and beak devoured my flesh each night
Until the Cuban workers came,
Turned the spoil of rent and rotted heart
Onto the newly planted sugarcane.

The Final Reasoning of Kings

On the parapet beyond my office door
Are six cannon from a distant war.
I can call them by their names,
Understand something of their range,
Their casting dates, the Latin of their kings:
Ultima Ratio Regum it reads on each of them.
On one side are *La Lézarde, Le Carillon*
On the other *Le Sévère, Le Tintamarre*
And in between, larger and more fatal,
If the comparative makes any sense,
Are *L'Envoi, L'Aurore.*
To come closer to this pair
Is to see two brass-green serpents crawl
Along the top of each toward the sighting beads;
Their arching backs provide the slots
By which they could be lifted into place.
One serpent of the four has lost its head,
Clapped off in need of shot,
Perhaps, or souvenir piece.
What does the added cost of casting such a whim
Tell us but how warfare was deemed partly art?
As for the names, when was it ever any different?
Achilles had his shield, Arthur his famous sword,
And any number of pilots a plane with wife's name.
Nor is the hint of wit here, in metaphor,
A particularly notable event.
After irony of ultimate reason is survival humor.

No sooner was the envoy's message gone
Than the other bore its light to dawn.
Then the wall-breaker, the little severe one,
The bell-ringer, the din.

No Fluid-Fed Governor

With my father I drive this low road
                    out into darkness
Where swamps press in
On what we have taken.
Beyond canals on either side
We hear the thrumming pulse of heavy diesels
Pumping water off the land.
In our nights they possess what comes within their pull—
We leave them unmanned—
Silent governors control the gravity flow
Of fuel from overhead tanks
And hold all needles below red line.

Miles back we left the highway,
Turned onto this road of crushed shell.
We follow its chalk whiteness,
Listening for the troubled engine.

Each pumping station we pass
Tells of its control
Over a share of this night's water.
Not until we are deep in the land,
                where the road begins
                    to give itself to swamp,
Do we find a diesel stalled.

It has ripped itself from the foundation,
Gone wild on fumes from an empty fuel tank—
                fumes no fluid-fed governor could command—

Some one of us allowed the fuel to run low;
By night the tank was emptied
Of all but vapor,
And vapor fed the wide-open chambers
That pushed all needles
        to red line and beyond.

Black earth is churned up
From the concrete pad to where
It lies like a broken animal,
        its small gauges
                fixed like eyes on the seashell road.

Options

Rank on rank of false right eyes
Stared into my loss
And I saw
He would not find my soft brown eye,
Not in a thousand leather trays;
Not for all the purple velvet
That could be cut to lay them on
Was there an option
Able to resplit my sight
Or make me a king.
Not even his costly Orientals
Could fake my lost right eye.

He tried, eye after eye;
They lay like bogus coins
In my forehead.

Level with his window was a minaret
On whose globe he said
To fix my fluid left eye
For a truer fit.
As he ground with sand and steel
To shape blown glass to my blind side,
I saw again the world no longer turned
Around the sun,
Was flat, lacked depth,
Went neither beyond
Nor came before
The one-dimensional plane

Of sky and globe and minaret.
Into that vacancy
He placed the cold brown eye
My father paid him money for.
It was like a slug in the music box;
I could not play my song.
When I reached for things
They still were not there.

In the mirror beside his window
I tried again to find a true brown eye;
The truest there
Was in my father's saddened face.
Through the dark prosthetic glass
Vision came of my sovereign option:
I broke from his hand,
The stranger's vitreous smile, that humorless room,
And went into the park below.
Bell notes floated from the minaret
Like concentric waves in the fountain pool
Where I threw the mold-blown piece
And began to sort the planes,
Play the songs,
Between sky and globe and minaret,
Trusting depth to the patch of black
Behind my lost brown eye.

THE MAJORETTE ON THE SELF-RISING FLOUR SIGN

She lay in tall grass behind the football field,
Twice again as large as any half-time majorette.
I don't remember who was the first, maybe Billy Gillette,
To kneel between her flaking thighs and pretend to smell
And then to lick, then dry hump as though he knew it all.
We all took our turns, hamming up a particular grasp
Or move we thought was cool, and then some smartass
Peeled the paint from around what he called her cock.
That's how much we knew, and you're thinking abuse
And gang rape in the making, and the obvious lack
Of education not to mention feeling, and that is right.
But what should also break our hearts is how we thought
That this was commodity the same as flour that could be bought.

JULY 4TH, 1960

Their fires
Still burn in memory
Across the lake
On Cypress Point:
We have our free ribs and beer
They theirs
On the other side
In the flickering
Other half of our company
Barbecue.
At the water's edge
I watch and hear
First song
Blues soul tonk
Then shouts
And know
There is blood
This 4th of July night
Even among their own.
Monday there will be a blue
And cut-up Negro
On the line.
We work in steam
And styrofoam
Side by side
At PolarTherm,
Make Santa Claus masks
And reindeer in July,
Surfboards and water jugs

In December,
But no styrofoam
That I might mold
Could seal or float
Me far enough
To where I could forget
Their fires
In jagged thin mirrors
On the water,
Not think of their lives
Separate from ours.

THE BIG MONEY COMES TO
MY HOMETOWN

They have done
well where I once
worked for minimum wage
on the graveyard
shift and learned the hours
of the Mississippi dark.
We made what served the leisure
public in its off-time hours—
ice buckets, camp stoves,
portable reclining chairs.
But the dies,
I read today,
are being cast
for different tempered steel.
The hometown paper says
POLARTHERM GETS
MULTI-MILLION DOLLAR
CONTRACT.   And in lowercase letters:
To Make Bomb Fins
For US Defense
Dep't.   Just as soon
as machines are retooled
from 100 to
200 additional persons will work my shift
for minimum wage
and learn to watch
the small, grave hours
of the dark.

THE BARBER WITH THE
CALIFORNIA TAN

California never saw a winter,
According to this barber at my back
Whose flagging leather long since ceased to temper
Any steel. His razor trembles at my neck.
Outside his window is a bogus barber pole
But signal nonetheless of former role,
Certified on little more than nerve,
When barbers let blood as purge and cure.

He claims an eternal California tan,
Says he went there once to harvest citrus fruit.
For proof he rolls the sleeve of his nylon barber suit
And bares the hairless white arm of an aging man.
When he is done and I have paid, I rise
And walk toward winter sunlight fragile as glass.

One Last Cheer for Punk Kincaid

We never believed that any judge's word
Could send Punk Kincaid to Parchman Farm,
But when Punk broke and wept
On the last night of his trial a year ago
We knew that he was guilty as accused
And never again would we run interference
As he brought back a downfield punt
Or took a hand-off on a sweeper play
And moved on out into an open field.
Today we are watching Negro trusties
Drag a lake near Parchman Farm
For his body.
Word had come that Punk went down
To help recover a drowned man;
We drove all morning into the Delta
Thinking he might rise grinning
Near the sidelines
And josh about this trick
He had pulled
Or simply say the names of towns
He cruised the rustled cattle through—
Anguilla, Rolling Fork, Redwood, on to Natchez—
And with the Negroes from the boat
Gathered with us in a circle
We would help him mile by mile
Through the outlaw past.
They drag the lake with net and hook
But it will not give him up—

Below their boat
The drowned are running interference
For Punk Kincaid
As he returns a punt
From deep inside his own territory.

No Doric Air

*I am prepared now and will be during the winter
period to take care of pupils in either Latin, Greek,
English, History, or Mathematics. The Mathematics
would embrace all grades from the 5th and 6th up
through the algebras, Plane Geometry, and
Trigonometry.*
    —A recent notice among the want ads of
    a southern small-town newspaper

By which Ionic foot, greater or lesser,
kind doctor, will you tame the southern *agricolae*
you see tomorrow bringing to your magnolia grove?

No Doric air stirs this Sunday afternoon,
these green waxen leaves shading fluted stone,
or the portico where, liveried in gray senility,
you wait to usher in the *tabulae rasae.*

From our air-conditioned Detroit car
we wave; you nod, thinking pupils have come early
to read of Xenophon's anabasis, Caesar's legions,
learn how *Gallia est omnis divisa in partes tres,*
and play that old Pythagorean rag.

The Pomegranate

I

It was to be no day of common fruit,
We knew, when Champ descended from his yellow bus
To schoolyard cinders,
Coming from out in the country,
      somewhere near the river,
Where each season yielded
     some new token
By which he held us to his slanted course.

No paper page was more read that morning
Than that of the large brown bag
In Champ's cubbyhole
      and none more blank.
But in our deepest body
We were waking to the votive stir
      of seed within seed.

Recess came and we entered
That random yard of cinders
Which today heard only our hushed voices
      and our beating blood.
We stood ready with common fruit
   to offer for a taste of pomegranate flesh.

With familiar hands
He plucked the crown of calyx lobes
And sank his fingers into the rind,
     opening to us the berried chambers

A summer heat had seeded.
Our hands went out, our blood caught and rose,
The strung wires of our nerves sang
                              a new wind,
And our teeth were set on edge
                    by small grenades of sweetness.

Seeing that more had come than could *have,*
Champ threw the remaining fruit into our midst
And took away
          our red and golden apples,
Leaving us with a lingering sweet acid taste
                              and cinders in our knees.

II

Before our chemistries surged us
              beyond his dazzling ciphers,
Before error forced us to trial,
We were locked further in the images of his lore:
After the pomegranate,
He muscled us with the dry ball of fur and bone
He brought to biology, a small hare
Regurgitated by the owl,
              and yet we are wiser
For having held the artifacts
That took shape in our hands
As he conjured out of mere traces
          a grotesque vision of the whole—the bleached snake
Bottled in alcohol,
          the egg it ate intact;

The viper eyes, the bulge, something our book
Could not rightfully illustrate.
Nor could it properly tell
The fragile mystery of the flying squirrel
        smothered in his unvented lard pail
Or of the hornet's nest we gave our lunch money for.

Drawn week by week
        into his rural sophistry,
Unable to break the stark analogies,
We were browbeat
Until we began to see into a world
        where the true word
Rarely found its rightful image.
That discovered, we began to cipher
The meaning of the expanding rebus
He drew.

Slowly most of us have come free
Of his twisted tales—of how hogs copulate
Or word of the literal "calm" that would flow
        from between the legs of manic backwood girls
    to warm him
Or any at the flush moment.
And yet how many sought in their souped-up coupes
        for that issue or some other impossibility of flesh
Long after he lost
        his grade-school hold?

Or seek still?—for it was no simple overthrow.
It is the images that most forcefully outlive
        their past,

Impending as he appears again,
        the ghost of a face home on leave,
Stoned on vodka,
      lost somewhere in the twistings of his own myth.
But in the snarl of memory
        a single vision
Defies his damages:
       one oblique morning
    when promise came of the seed's fruition.

Languages We Are Not Born To

Can we hear with a different ear the sounds
That bolted from your inarticulate jaw,
Can we call back our laughter
That burned your eyes to salt,
Now that you speak in another tongue
And make of speech a song?

You came with fractious talk
          from a broken mobile home
And tried with maladroit tongue to answer questions
Posed in the language that those around you spoke,
Tried until you learned that languages we are born to
          are not always our own.

Having stumbled into a foreign tongue
And stilled the stutter
That broke your native speech,
Can you give us now some word
To quiet the flutter
Which works unheard
On our own hidden lips and tongues?

CIRCLING THE REEF

Searching without charts for the fertile reef,
we prowl beyond sight
         of land or boat,
our depth-recorder
tuned to sound and graph
the vast erratic pulse of earth's relief.
The steady rise of the needle line
         on its unreeling cylinder
slows us to a troll, and making circles
                  we pull our silver lures
      through the blue heart of time
where blood schools in its deepest dream.

KELLY DUG A HOLE

I set the stakes,
Stretched the twine,
Told my labor crew
How deep, how wide to go,
Told them not to twist
Or bend their holes,
Not to bring them
To a point or flare
Because we'd have
To have the bottoms
Square and flat
To pour the footings
Where a building
Would finally stand.
Other workers flared,
Caved in the walls,
Or bent theirs
Out of shape,
But Kelly dug
And kept his straight,
Dug fifteen feet
Into a hill
The dozer missed.
When Kelly got on grade
I dropped the plumb
To check his hole.
At the top
I held the string
Three inches from the edge;

Down below
The plumb bob
Ceased its swing
Three inches from the wall
And told me
Kelly's hole was true.
We built in ice and heat;
We built a building
Five stories high
In Oxford, Mississippi.
The walls and floors
Are spider-cracked in places
From some slight shifting,
But the building stands
And if any part will hold
When things begin
To slide and fall
That part will be
Where Kelly dug his hole.

Epilogue

DEEP IN DORDOGNE

There is a human cave
I once inhabited
for part of a morning
on a limestone bluff
deep in Dordogne.
Other rooms were vacant
in the town far below
at the Hôtel Cro-Magnon,
but I wanted to sit on the racial floor
where our home had been of necessity
both hearth and window in one.
I wanted to look out over the river
where game once came to water
and fish swam
toward our earliest tables.
When we were barely lingual
there was a view
to the edgy tree line
of holm oak and walnut,
and I tried to imagine fear and need
so deep I would dig into rock
with nothing but another rock
and then rest and bring fire
from below and eat
what I gathered and reach up higher
to begin another cave above
this, to chip away again with my rock
toward what I hoped
would be a safer, higher loft,

toward architecture and furniture,
toward mathematics and an instrument
for my song.
But another form like mine
is coming from beneath the understory
of oak and nut tree,
and I must decide if he can climb
with his club to my room,
and for what:
my food, my fur of aurochs,
my daughter he has tracked
with his one syllable?
Or to hear these words
I am working toward song?